CW01612565

Publisher - English Churches Housing Group

Printed by Printwise (Haverhill) Limited, Haverhill, Suffolk

With special thanks to the following:
Roy Brazier of the Haverhill & District Local History Group,
Technical support from Lester Milbank & Derek Bruce of Cambridge Film & Television Productions Ltd,
Barry Young, Richard Urwin, Philip Laver

and a special thank you to all those who made this book possible.

Further Information from The Cangle: 01440 715400

English Churches Housing

Making the difference for people in need

St Edmundsbury
BOROUGH COUNCIL

PRO BONO PUBLICO

HAVERHILL TOWN COUNCIL

Help the Aged

Help the Aged
Millennium Awards

CONTENTS

INTRODUCTION

The Cangle School stood empty for many years and was falling into disrepair which concerned many people. St Edmundsbury Borough Council ran a competition with a specific brief designed to meet housing need and to find a new use and conserve the building. English Churches Housing Group was chosen to develop a groundbreaking scheme, in partnership with the Local Authorities and Laing Partnership homes.

The Cangle Foyer, a mixed housing development of general needs and supported housing with community facilities, (including a cyber café and IT training suite) has been developed.

It was important not to lose all the collective memories of the School over the years. St Edmundsbury Borough Council, Haverhill Town Council and English Churches Housing Group set up a Reminiscence Project which was funded by the Councils and Help the Aged Millennium Awards. Many local schools were involved in interviewing a range of staff and pupils from the old school with the help of Reminiscence workers. A piece of history is now captured in this publication.

THE CONTRIBUTORS

Derek Bacon, a policeman's son travelled from Kedington to the school with four friends when he was 11 in 1940. He left aged 14 to get a job.

Ted Basham started school in 1915 aged 4 with his sister. He left in 1925 and started work at Gurteen's factory in Haverhill where he worked all his life.

Diane Basham was at Cangle school from age 4 to age 15 in 1945 and lived in Haverhill near the school.

Roy Brazier attended Cangle School, then called Haverhill Secondary Modern between 1948 and 1951. He is now Vice Chairman of The Haverhill and District Local History Group.

Karen Clark started school in 1966 when she was 4. She came from London with her parents and sister. Karen left Cangle aged 11 and went on to Parkway School for the next 5 years. Karen has left Haverhill.

Susan Dockery is the last person to have ever taught at the old Cangle, still teaching at the new Cangle.

Jane Duffy went to nursery school aged 4 in 1976 with her brother. She lives and works locally.

Gladys Ely (neé Plum) started school in 1939. She still lives in Haverhill. When she left school she worked at the District Council next door to the school.

Jane Farrow (neé Ager) was at the school between 1965 and 1971. Her mother and Grandmother were dinner ladies at Cangle. Jane also attended Chalkstone school and later became a school teacher in Haverhill where she lives today.

Hilary Filben attended the school from 1947 aged 5 for ten years. She remembers a reunion held recently when everyone aged 50 had a get together. Hilary stayed at Cangle with her brother while her sister moved on to the grammar school in Sudbury.

Val Gagen started Cangle school in 1941 when he was 13. He lived at Hundon, a long bike ride to and from school each day. He left aged 15 and later joined the RAF.

Marion Gregory is a teacher and was acting deputy head on several occasions. She joined old Cangle in 1967, had a short break to complete teacher training and then stayed till the school closed down in 1987.

Alan Haigh taught at the school as the Head of Science and Mathematics Departments from 1958 to 1971 then became deputy head of Castle Hill all middle school in Haverhill and Head of the Arnold Middle school in Bedfordshire. He now lives in Somerset.

Christine Hart lived opposite the school and was 4½ when she started in 1950. She left in 1956 for Sudbury Grammar School at the age of 11.

Reg Herrington lived in Kedington and attended the school with several friends from the same village from 1941. He later joined the Fire service and now lives in Gloucestershire.

Jean Howlett was at Cangle for one year after being abroad with her parents. Her Father was stationed at Wratting Common Air Base.

Gerry Kiernan started at Cangle in 1970 having just arrived in Haverhill from London. He is now a Councillor with St Edmundsbury Borough Council.

Cyril Nunn started school aged 5 in 1928 and left when he was 14. He used to be a poacher.

Peter Isaacs went to Cangle in 1955 aged 5. He has always lived in Haverhill.

Jean and Robert (Bob) Pavely were both born in Haverhill and both attended Cangle school. Their friend Muriel Moore (Neé scott) was born in the town also.
Bob started Cangle in 1933 aged 5. His parents and brothers had also attended. Jean and Muriel joined a few years later.

Rose Phillips started school aged 5 in 1919 and used to have lunch each day at her Grandma's who lived nearby.

Gwen Salmon was at Cangle school during the war from 1940 until she left in 1946 aged 14. She cycled to school from Great Thurlow whatever the weather.

Geoffrey Ship lived close to the school and attended age 5 to 11. He left in 1963 to go to a much bigger school 20 miles away. He is now a teacher.

Julie Smith went to Cangle school aged 9, in 1972 for about a year after moving to Haverhill from London as part of the over-spill population. Her husband joined at about the same time.

Hazel Smith joined the staff in 1953 at a time when most teachers at the school were men. She went on part-time after getting married and left when Castle Manor School had opened.

Percy Sizer went to school in 1921 with his brothers and sisters. He left in 1930 when he was 14 and worked at Gurteen's for over 50 years. He has lived in Haverhill all his life.

Harold Sozer was born in Gt Dunmow during the First World War and came to Haverhill when he was 1 year old. He started school aged 4 and left aged 14 in 1930. Harold also worked at Gurteen's.

Tony Stevens was at Cangle School from age 11 in 1948 to 1951. He lived on a farm at Helions Bumpstead about 3 miles from Haverhill and still lives and works on the farm today.

Michael Teedale was a pupil at the school in 1950 when he was aged 11 having been at a local village primary school nearby.

Beryl Wade's grandfather helped build the school in 1877. Her mother and three brothers went to the school and Mrs Wade attended in 1929 until she was 14. Her daughter and grandchildren followed in her footsteps. Mrs Wade also worked at the school as ancillary classroom helper and nurse. Her husband **Albert Wade** was caretaker there for 7 years after being in the building trade. They are now retired but still live almost opposite the school.

With special thanks to everyone who shared their memories and memorabilia with present day pupils and their teachers at Reminiscence events over the past year.

FIRST IMPRESSIONS

I can just remember the first day at school, my mother taking me there, and lots of little children all crying and holding their mother's hands. Then we sat round little tables and chairs as they do now, I suppose. We were shown the corridor where we all had to hang our coats, the little row of toilets outside and the canteen.

Hilary Filben

I can remember my first day and the person I sat next to, which was Barry Basham, and I can remember he had a lunchbox. The rest, a lot of it, is blank. My teacher was Miss Martin.

Peter Isaacs

I remember this kindly teacher, like a second mum, called Miss Large, I don't think she was a large lady. We used to go in a more central doorway when we started, because the infants school there was a hall on the left, there was an inner cloakroom with a row of washbasins with the toilets outside. There must have been more than one infant class, and it was all within the same area, and we all shared the same cloakroom. I can remember it being a large classroom, but what we did in that classroom I haven't got an idea.

Diane Basham

I remember my first teacher was Miss Large. She was a very nice woman. I also remember that I was the youngest of a little gang and they'd all gone to school before me. I wanted to be there with them. I was always a class behind, but I didn't want to be left out.

Jean Pavely

The first day I was there was actually a school trip to Colchester Zoo. I was given the opportunity of starting school a bit later rather than go into school that day, but I'd thought I'd go along. I knew no-one, and sat on the bus all by myself with my packed lunch. It's quite a vivid memory.

Julie Smith

My first day was quite frightening because it was all very new and I had to get on a bus at home early in the morning and come by bus and then we arrived at the school and it was a very big school because the school I'd been to only had three classes and this was a very big school and there were lots of people that I'd didn't know and I was 11 and some people were 15 and so there were lots of very big people there as well.

Michael Teedale

The first thing I remember about is just how big it was when I was very little. There were lots of different rooms, lots of different corridors, I wasn't sure that I would be able to find my way around. I think that's the first thing I remember, coming from a little house into a big building, just how big it was.
I can remember somebody who I met on the first day, he was a boy called Adrian Withers. We still send each other a Christmas card, and keep in touch even after 40 years.

Geoffrey Ship

I don't remember feeling frightened until I was about 8 and we had a teacher that was really nasty, I really didn't like her at all. I can remember my father dragging me screaming down the High street to go to school because I disliked the woman so much. But I had to go, there wasn't any other choice.

Christine Hart

I was a bit apprehensive on my first day. I started going to the village school at Kedington, this was before the days when they moved older children on to other schools. You normally stayed at the village school all the time. But my parents thought that I should improve my education by going to Haverhill. There were several of us from Kedington went, about four or five of us. It was purely voluntary, our parents sent us there because they thought it was better for us. There was John Gower, Derek Bacon, Tony Maize, that's the three from Kedington. There was a chap called Reg Herrington who lived at Calford Green which was quite near to Kedington. School times were pleasant, although we probably didn't think so at the time.

Val Gagen

I was quite happy that I was going to a school with my brother until I actually got outside the gates and I can remember crying and mum said I was like that for a couple of days. I can only remember the first day being a little bit upset. Just going to school and leaving my mum, I think, more than anything.
The first year you were at the front of the school, with a separate play areas. So the first year, if you're looking at the Cangle School, you play in the right hand side and when you're in the second year, you play on the left hand side of the playground. The third and fourth years were at the back, in front of the dining area, but they could actually play in the same sort of area. It was sectioned off as such, you just knew that that wasn't your area. It was safer really. We quite liked being in our little huddles.

Jane Duffy

GETTING TO SCHOOL

Three boys in the village and myself found that we were on the transfer list for Haverhill, this was in 1940.
There was no transport facilities so this meant that to get there we would have to cycle anyway. My cycle had quite a history. It was a ladies model and it belonged to the daughter of a very prominent person in the village who in fact shot his daughter, his wife and then committed suicide. This was the bike that was going to take me for the next three years backwards and forwards to Haverhill.
It was about a three mile journey. It's difficult now to remember a lot about it, but I think in the main we enjoyed it. We all lived in the village, we all had bicycles so there was no real problem. Wintertime was not so good, but we didn't seem to bother anyway. Being youngsters you had a far different attitude then to what people do today, you just got on with it.

Derek Bacon

Withersfield Road c1900 *From a collection of old postcards*

I used to come down with another girl that lived up on the farm, and they had a pony and cart, and they used to bring us down every morning in this little pony and cart, the three of us, and drop us off outside the school. Then pick us up and take us back up to Wolesey.

Rose Philips

I used to walk to school from Ash Grove where we lived. At the back of my garden where I lived then was all countryside. It's all built up now. I never used to be taken to school, I always walked, all the kids did. When I was at the new school in the seniors, we had to walk back to the Cangle to do woodwork.

Peter Isaacs

The school entrance at that time of day was just at the bottom of Wratting Road, next door to where the headmaster lived. I went in there hand in hand with a girl named Nancy Bowman.
Some of the farmers in the little villages, they used to bring their children in on a horse and cart to get a better education. There were no cars about really, we saw perhaps one car a week. I remember there being a petrol station down on the corner, Hayward's Garage, it was 1s 10d a gallon then.

Harold Sozer

Everybody walked to school. There was no public transport in Haverhill. Most of us didn't have cycles, but I remember that Thelma had a three wheeler bike. I never had a cycle until I was eleven, which was after I had passed for the high school. Although my family didn't have any money I saved up. I used to run errands for my grandmother's cousin who was a dressmaker when I was ten-ish. I used to get paid 3d a week and I used to go to one lady who was the wife of the man who run the bus company, Burgeons, and she would give me six pence.

I should think it was about 3/4 of a mile, and would have taken us nearly ten minutes. Of course there wasn't much traffic on the roads, and there was only one major employer which was Gurteen's factory.

The Old School 1958 *Alain Haigh*

Diane Basham

Most people walked to school then. They used to gather together. You know the modern thing that they call a walking bus? It's come to the fore in East Anglia a little while ago. All the children collect together with a couple of mums and they all have yellow tabards on, and they walk to school. We didn't have that sort of organisation but the older ones always had to take the younger ones. That was the recognised thing that you all went to school together. But there wasn't the worry in those days.

Jean Pavely

I lived not far from the school and you could just run to the school on your own. There was no traffic to be aware of or anything like that. The school bell used to ring about ten to nine and you could hear it most all of the place, it was so loud. Then you'd have the monitors, or the prefects, on the door and they took down all the names of the children that were late. If you were late more than two or three times a week you got into trouble.

A lot of the children came from the villages as well. We had all the surrounding villages because the Cangle was probably the only school for miles around. We had the buses come in with all the village children. But we all got on very well. There weren't fights or anything like that.

Hilary Filben

High Street c1930 *From a collection of old postcards*

Coming from out of town we arrived by bus each day more or less the same time as one of the teachers on a small motorcycle. One morning he followed our transport to school and the boys in the rear seats gave him the V for victory sign, but the wrong way round. We thought we had got away with it as nothing was said all day, but as we assembled in the classroom to catch our homeward bus, in came the offended teacher. "Who was it who offered me rude remarks?" he boomed. No one owned up for a while and were kept waiting for over half an hour before we thought better of it and confessed in order to get home that night.

Roy Brazier

I lived on the Parkway estate, as my parents still do, which is quite a way from the School. My mum took me for a few months at the beginning, and after that I went on the bus. So from the age of 5 or 6 I was on the school bus. In fact the bus conductor actually recognised me a couple of years ago when I was in Cambridge.
It was safe, there wasn't as much traffic and I used to be able to get to school on my own.

Karen Clark

THE NAME OF THE SCHOOL

When I was there, I'm sure it wasn't called the Cangle School, it was the Haverhill School. Well, I suppose being the only school we just said we've got to go to school so it was just the Haverhill School.

Gladys Ely

View of the Cangle c1901 *From a collection of old postcards*

It was called the Cangle within the last 3 or 4 decades. After the war I think it was still the Council School.

We had a secondary school there as well, it wasn't just the Cangle now I come to think about it. It was the boys school, the girls school and the secondary. The secondary was this end, the boys was that end and the girls was sort of in the middle. We had to take a secondary exam. I went in for it and I passed it, but you weren't forced to go and I wouldn't go. I didn't like boys. So I stayed at Cangle until I was 14. Then after a while the secondary school closed and they used to travel to Sudbury if you passed a certain exam.

Beryl Wade

I don't know why it's called the Cangle. We've always known it as the Cangle, it was the Cangle when I went there. But that was the only school in my day anyway.

Gwen Salmon

It was called the Cangle School when I was there, it always was. They call Broad Street the Cangle. If people lived in Broad Street you used to say they lived up the Cangle. I think it's something to do with that being a dead end.

Percy Sizer

When my father went there, it was called the Board School. Then when I went to school it was called the Council School. It's only recently they've called it the Cangle School. I think they changed it in the 1960's, I think. It was called the Council School when I was there.

Harold Sozer

The name Cangle comes from a piece of land on the 1737 tythe map. The Headmaster chose the name accordingly. The design of the badge could be 'C' in an angle which was easy to reproduce.

Jean Pavely

Trough outside Cangle c1905 *From a collection of old postcards*

We just called it the Cangle, I don't know what its official title was. It was the main one in the town, everyone went there.

Julie Smith

At the time of my arrival as a teacher in Haverhill in January 1958, the school was not known as 'Cangle'. The Withersfield Road site housed both the Primary School and the Modern Secondary School, as established under the 1944 Education Act. For some reason, West Suffolk had chosen the title "Haverhill Modern Secondary School" rather than the more usual "Secondary Modern", though I suppose it is, on reflection, probably grammatically more correct. The old Grammar School had long departed, to become amalgamated with Sudbury Grammar School, and I believe that they had originally occupied part of the western end of the buildings now housing the Secondary School, under the leadership of Mr Underwood. The Primary School was in the eastern end of the site, under the headship of Miss Potter. The name 'Cangle' was given to the school by Mr Hutchinson a year or two later, when the whole building became the Primary School and he was appointed Head. He did some research into local history and this part of Haverhill had been connected with the name.

Alan Haigh

I just knew it as the Cangle. They closed that one and named another school after it. It just doesn't click, I don't associate it with that. Cangle is Cangle, the big school on that corner and that's always Cangle. I don't even know where the new Cangle is actually, but it's just not right, it's not the Cangle.

Karen Clark

Secondary School Pupils 1958 *Alan Haigh*

THE BUILDING

I remember the old stone floors and, as my daughter said she remembers, sitting on the wooden floors and getting splinters in your pants. The class rooms were divided up by folding doors, so they divided off into classrooms when you needed them and for assemblies they pulled back and there was a big hall. The rooms were very small compared to today's schools. I can remember the Head's office, it was a very small one.

Gladys Ely

The building had very high ceilings because it's a Victorian building and very big windows in it. The corridors were quite wide and the doors were very big. The room that we were in when I was in the final year had dividers across it so you could pull it across and shut it up and make it into two rooms. Otherwise it was quite a big room, wooden floors. It was quite a labyrinth really, because there were a lot of classrooms all the way around and I think the building was shaped like an 'E'. It had two wings, except it hadn't got the middle piece. You went in at the front on the long side and the classroom that I was finally in was the one that is on the right as you stand looking at the front of the building now, that last one there. When we started we went to the other side. Miss Potter's office was in the left hand side and that's where we used to go when we had needlework.
I think the Cangle is such a lovely building. I just love Victorian buildings, there is something so solid and dependable and yet at the same time so imaginative about them.

Christine Hart

The entrance was where the contractors today go in and out. To the left of that was Percy Underwood's office. The building there, that was the first building. I think there was a corridor. 3A was then at slightly right angles to that, which would then be facing the Rose & Crown, if you can imagine that. 2B would have been the corridor and then the other side would have been either 1A or 1B. Then as you went back the other classes were further in. There was a large hall where we had tea and things like dancing, that sort of thing, and singing of course.

Derek Bacon

I was very interested in the Cangle as a building, being in the building trade. I realised it was built in the days when there was a lot of skill in building.
It was built in the 1870's by a firm called Masons, they did a lot of the big buildings in Haverhill. The actual brickwork was of very high quality, it uses what they call herringbone brickwork. I believe it was built in the days when men used to go home

quite happy and satisfied with their day's work.
I remember once, they were losing a lot of water. One weekend I had to shut down all the water inside the school and then check with a water meter outside. I'd shut the water meter down and then they would know whether they were losing water with all the services shut inside the school. That meant I had to more or less lay down on the path to check a water meter. Then I had to do it again on the Monday morning. It so happened that I was laying down on the path checking the water meter and a motorist went by and thought I'd collapsed. They actually called an ambulance and the ambulance came and of course I'd gone!
In 1977 the school was a hundred years old. On the front of the school there was a stone plaque stating when it was built and all the names of those when it was first planted there. I restored it so that it stood out for the 100 year centenary. It's still there now.

Albert Wade

Haverhill board schools 1884 *Taken from a leaflet*

To me, the building was very big. The pegs seemed very high. I can remember in one of the assembly rooms that used to have a divider in between it, so that if it was just a classroom assembly they'd put the divider in so it was just a small area.
If it was for the whole school then they would take that partition back and it just seemed like a massive, massive room. Now, if you go and have a look at it, it just seems so tiny, how could all these people fit in there?
My favourite classroom was my first year. I remember it being very light and airy in there and the toilets were just outside. Where we were in my last year of school, it was right next to the dinner hall and that always seemed to very noisy.

Jane Duffy

The Building was cold, with very high windows. School buildings today, every child can see out of the window and see what's happening. But in the old buildings the windows were high and therefore there was no gazing out of the window. I had one of the classrooms along the front of the building, towards the Broad Street end, and it was the middle one of the three, and it was used for assembly. There were three rooms we used for assembly, once or twice a week, and we had these big screens that folded back, and the caretaker used to come in and convert it all in to one big room and then we had to sit and wait. Three teachers sharing the room until he came back after assembly to put it all back again.

Hazel Smith

The one thing I can remember are the tin sheds at the back and the playground.

Rose Philips

The building was all brick, there was no plasterwork. The bricks were painted over. Years ago, they used to have big, old fires and then we had big, old, iron radiators with huge pipes that went round the school. You used to have to cock your leg over the pipes to go into the next classroom in some of the rooms.

Percy Sizer

We used to have these big windows with blinds up. One of the things we used to do, if your friend was sitting one end of the class and I was sitting at the other, we used to write little notes and then tie them on the cords on the blinds and swing them to each other. We had some good fun there.

I do remember the fountain; they call it the horse trough now, don't they? But I can always remember it as the fountain. We used to meet up there, a crowd of us, and then go off into school.

It smelt in the canteen, because the cooking area was so close to the dining area. It was in a little side building off the school. You used to go up little steps at the top of the playground into this white building. You used to have to have sittings, of course, because it wasn't a very big room. If you were second or third sitting there wasn't much left at all.

Hilary Filben

My first classroom was actually in the main building with old, high windows. It was quite dark I remember. In the second year we were in a prefab building further away that you to go upstairs to get to. That's been knocked down, it wasn't part of the actual building that's been left. It was probably more substantial than a prefab. I remember it having corrugated iron in various parts.

It's the building thing, the old, not quite musty but sort of a woody smell, mixed with like powder paint. Every now and again I've been somewhere and you smell something and it takes you right back to your schooldays. It might be polish, something like that. I can't remember where I was recently but I remember being thrown right back to the changing rooms with these really low coat pegs.

Julie Smith

School showing fountain 1912 *History Group*

Along Withersfield Road there is a little bit that looks like a house, and that used to be the caretakers house. But Mr Ince was not living there when I came, he'd already given that up, and that was used for the offices. The staff room was up above. The School was originally built to have the caretaker and the head living on the block. There was always the traipse across the yard for some of the classrooms which were outside, and for the dining room also.

There were the two buildings, the woodwork shop and the metalwork shop, which I understand had been part of the old Vit-Hovis complex at one time. They were the ones right at the back by the driveway. There were two other prefab type of classrooms in the yard as well, so if you were working in any of those you obviously had to go outside to get to them.

Hazel Smith

I can sort of remember the layout of the school. As you come in the front gate there was the infants and there were the horse chestnuts either side in the playground. The main entrance to the school was in front. If I remember rightly, the headmaster's office and the administration office was there on the right hand side, and the nurse was there. As you went it, it opened up into the cloakroom and further along there were toilets, they may have been outside, I can't remember.

The left hand side went through to the big hallway. There was another hallway the other side, but I think that one was classrooms. The actual hall that we used for assemblies was on the right hand side. There was definitely the cloakroom there and then there was a door sort of in front. Perhaps there was some sort of sink area that was there. There was something to do with water in that corner. I can't remember whether the toilets were outside or in. My coat peg was on the back wall as you come through the door. There were some here and then there were some along the wall and mine was at the back.

I like Victorian buildings anyway and you can still see what was originally the boy/girl entrances and things like that, because you've got the two doors one each side. That little area is still very much as it was. You've got all the old houses next to it and Broad Street that goes up, that's all still the Victorian houses. Then you've got the Corn Exchange right opposite which is the original building as well. So the actual buildings around the school from a certain angle are still very much the same.

There were quite big classrooms, old big windows and stuff like that, the arched windows which were quite nice. You don't appreciate it at the time.

Karen Clark

The classroom when I was with Mr Roy was the one that was right at the very back, made out of corrugated tin next to the kiln. You had to go up the steps to get to this classroom. It was rather a nice, big classroom. I think we were quite privileged to have the kiln. I can remember it being a small, square room but very tall. You'd look up and there'd be lumps of clay that had somehow attracted themselves to the ceiling. The dining hall was at the back of the school. It wasn't a red brick building. It was quite a hideous building really. That seemed fairly bleak. Assemblies were held in there sometimes.

Jane Farrow

It was built in 1876 because the Government passed a law in 1870 which said that there had to be a school in every town, and in the next few years after 1870 lots and lots of schools were built, so I think it was built in 1876. I think it closed about 10 years ago, so it would be about 1987, 1988.

We used to have the hall, which used to be made into three classrooms, that always used to seem very big. I suppose they weren't that much different to the size of the classrooms today, but there were more children in the class so they were a bit more crowded really and we used to sit in desks, not on tables. So you had to sit with one other person, you had desks that held two people.

I seem to remember there were toilets and sinks and cloakrooms altogether with classrooms around them, in a square from what I can remember. I think you had like three or four classrooms that were sort of dotted around the toilets and a very big cloakroom, so everybody hung their coats in one big cloakroom, well not everybody, but about 100 people or so and then there were toilets in with the cloakrooms and then classrooms sort of round the edge of it from what I can remember.

The school from Wratting Road 1912 (just before First World War) *History Group*

They used to use a kind of polish on the floors that didn't smell very nice, that funny sort of polishy smell. And sometimes cloakrooms had that sweaty smell after a lot of people got changed from PE.

Some of the classrooms were built as temporary classrooms during the war and they weren't as strong as the other ones. They had tin roofs like you get on sheds, corrugated iron, so we weren't all in the main part of the school, we weren't all in the brick part of the school. They were built in World War II, because in the war there weren't very many building materials around, so they built very cheaply, thinking that when the war was over they'd build better classrooms but it never got changed, so they were still there 20 years after the war when I was there.

Geoffrey Ship

We had gas lights in the building, there was no electric then. We didn't get the facilities like they get now.

Percy Sizer

The building smelt mouldy sometimes after a holiday, if it was damp, and you would go in and it would smell mouldy and in the TV room, children used to sit on the carpet and the warmth of their bodies used to make all the dampness come up through the floor, it used to leave like little puddles of water on the carpet.

Susan Dockery

When I first went for the interview, like I say, it was a serious step for me to take because most of my time here I was a bricklayer. To take the caretaker's job was quite a drop financially. But when I thought about it, I was going to be right near the school and my main hobby is gardening and I was going to have a certain amount of time off during the day. So I decided to try for the position, which I was successful. But I always remember the superintendent of caretakers, he approached me afterwards and said, "What I would like to tell you is, this is a very happy school and that is the way we want to keep it". I spent several happy years there really. I was the father to them all! I had a good relationship with them.
They gave me quite a bit of a celebration really. When I had to retire I did enjoy being there and it was quite a sad day when I had to leave really. But being a local authority, they were very strict on leaving on the age of 65.

Albert Wade

THE CLOCK

The clock being there was one of the things that everybody in the town at some time or the other must have looked at and thought Oh God it's late. That and the church clock were the two that we always used to go by but I can remember the school clock always used to work, because it's part of the building really, isn't it?

Gladys Ely

I'm very interested in clocks. I do a lot of clock restoration myself. It did strike and it was a fine clock. I don't know who's repairing it this time or indeed if it has been repaired. It was a wonderful old thing. I'm very keen on that type of clock .

Derek Bacon

I know the man who wound the clock, Mr Wade. I don't remember him doing it, I only knew about this later because I didn't know him then. Albert Wade is his name, and he was the caretaker at the school, so I did see him about when I was there. But I only really got to know him years later, he actually lived behind us when we lived in that little row of houses, he still lives there now. I didn't ever see him winding the clock. But he continued to do it long after the building was closed.

Christine Hart

The Clock Tower *Printwise*

I used to have to wind the clock up twice a week. It meant getting a ladder, it was up in a trapdoor and it was just inside on the outside doors. I always used to have to bolt the door, put the ladder up to the trapdoor and to wind the clock you stood on the trapdoor which you had opened, that was such a small space. It kept good time. It was serviced every year by Smiths, the clock people. Although it stopped for a while, it's almost going again. It's going to be on automatic winder now. I thought they might call me back to see how it was wound up, but I believe that's all altered now, it's going to be automatic. When the school closed, I done it on a voluntary basis, I kept the clock going. Unfortunately, after a time the school was entered and vandalised quite a lot so I was advised to stop doing it and the clock had to stop because there was a danger.

Albert Wade

THE BELL

Mr Ince the caretaker used to ring a bell in the mornings. I was in lodgings on the other side of town and I think he used to ring this bell, whether it was at quarter to nine or whether it was at five to, I really don't remember. But he used to stand in the doorway under the clock and pull the rope, and when this bell started to ring you'd see children running from all directions because they knew that it was time that they should be in, which is something that doesn't happen anywhere anymore.
He got to know the children particularly well, he would know who was late because he'd ring this bell, and his wife used to be one of the cleaners. They were a real sort of team.

Hazel Smith

I was never late I don't think. I think if we were late you got sent to Mr Underwood but I never was late. I think my Auntie used to make sure of that and of course wherever you lived in the town you weren't what you'd call really far from school. They used to ring the bell when you get in the school grounds playing way, so I think wherever you were you heard and thought Oh God were late. That was something, I remember the school bell ringing and the school clock.

Gladys Ely

There was a bell on the top of the building and there were hand bells too that they used to ring when you had to come in from the playground.

Christine Hart

I remember we used to have a lot of fire drills and what have you. My dad was a fireman in Haverhill at the time so I thought that was really great that my dad came. The bell used to go, we all had to get out the classrooms and we had to stand in a straight line in classrooms and we all had a set area to stand in the playground which we all knew we had to. The firemen were there just to basically say how well we did. I can remember them coming quite often to the school and gave us talks as well about things. It used to be the whole school in the back playground but not one word was ever muttered. All these children being so well behaved just because this bell had gone off.
It was the only time it ever happened with all of us being quiet. I can remember my dad coming one day and I was told off by the teacher because my dad was trying to do his job and I got all giggly and silly and she said I must stand up straight and be quiet.

Jane Duffy

I can remember doing a handstand just after the bell went and I got told off for that. I was upside down up against the wall and the bell had just gone and I was caught.

Karen Clark

Mr Scrivener was a very stern man, wasn't he? He was the caretaker.
He would stand underneath the little tower where the clock is and he'd got a cord coming down that would strike the same bell that the clock rings. He'd never let anyone else ring it.

Jean Pavely

THE TOILETS

The toilets were outside, very primitive. You always had to go outside to go to the loo, no matter what the weather was like. They were; awful, smelly, cold and wet. Sometimes boys used to lay in wait for you outside and pelt you when you came out, especially if there was snow on the ground. And you only had that really hard toilet paper, but they still have that in schools now.

Christine Hart

They were the old Victorian ones with a little row of sinks, real tiny ones. There were two, there was a boys' toilets and the girls' toilets.

Beryl Wade

I do remember one instance when I wanted to go to the toilet and the prefect wouldn't let me back in so I sat on the step and I wet my knickers. They sorted me out and gave me a clean pair of knickers and sent me home with the wet ones. My mum wasn't very impressed, she went down and complained because I should have been allowed to go to the loo. I don't know if there was a policy change after that, I'm not really sure. I think it was because it was this prefect thing and they were older and they thought they could boss the infants around type of thing.

Karen Clark

There used to be lots of little walls behind the toilets where you could go and hide when you were playing hide and seek, so there used to lots of little nooks and crannies, lots of hiding places when you were playing games of chase or hide and seek where you could hide away, so I used to quite like all the little corners.

Geoffrey. Ship

The outside toilets were always a knotty problem because in the wintertime we used to have shut them down, shut the main supply of water down and go round and flush every toilet until it was empty. In spite of that, they did get frozen up at different times, which presented quite a problem. The pipes burst sometimes as well. You could easily get caught out, if you happened to forget to shut them down, or if you weren't appear that it was going to be severe, if you didn't shut them down of course you were in serious trouble because you'd have a row of solid toilets, solid water.

Albert Wade

HEATING THE SCHOOL

As the caretaker, I used to get down there about half past six of a morning and put the heat on. That was another problem, heat, because the building had so many external doors. It used to warm up alright up until nine o'clock, but once the doors started to open they used to have a heat problem with all the open doors.
The boiler was timed to come on at a certain time in the morning. It was an oil fired boiler. If it broke down, I used to have to phone the engineers and that used to present problems. I wasn't on very good terms with the teachers then.

Albert Wade

Originally the school all had open fires. We had the big ones in the centre of the classrooms, the old combustion things, and they used to be made up with coal and that, when I went there, and coke mostly because it was cheaper. They were safe because they had this huge stove in the middle of the classroom with the pipe going through the ceiling, but they had a big guard around it. They were called tortoise stoves. They were really efficient heat-wise, because they used to stand in the middle and all the heat would come out.

Beryl Wade

Hugh Ince was the caretaker when I was teaching at the school. He was quite a character as well. He of course stoked the old coke boiler in those days. There was a lot of dust and grime about the place that came from that, and the school floors were those wooden blocks, which he treated with oil in the holidays. I suppose it must have been to lay the dust, but I know the impression was on your hemlines, if you had anything light coloured you would have this black mark eventually. All the floors seemed to be black and grimy, but it was this oil that did it.

Hazel Smith

We were never cold in that school, were we? They had great big pipes and big radiators. The caretaker, Mr Scrivener used to have a stoke hole at the back there. He had the knowledge of that heating system down to a fine art. We were never cold in school and yet he couldn't have had unlimited supplies of fuel because nobody could get fuel, could they, not in the war?

Jean Pavely

It wasn't cold in the school. They had a boiler, the caretaker had a house in between the secondary school and the infants school. They had the boilers at the back and they had radiators all in the classrooms. They were coke boilers. They didn't smell. The radiators heated the hot water from the boilers at the back.

Harold Sozer

My arrival as a teacher, in midwinter, was accompanied by some particularly cold weather, which made great demands upon the antiquated and creaking central heating system of the school. The boiler was situated in a large cellar under a classroom at the middle of the back of the school, with access down a ladder from the playground. It was controlled (insofar as it was possible to be controlled) by the Caretaker, Tom Ince, and his assistant, with whom I got on very well, Ron Jacobs. The boiler was constructed of separate large cast-iron sections, bolted together to make a boiler of the requisite size, but due to its advanced age, the ravages of the hardness of the local water supply and its tendency to overheat, sections had already burnt out and been removed. New replacement sections were not always readily available, so it was a matter of replacing with second hand sections as, when and if they became available. Each time a section was taken out, the capacity was reduced, and the poor old boiler was really struggling.

About two weeks into the term, on a particularly cold night, the boiler uttered its last gasp, and morning inspection revealed that it had burnt out a section, sprung a leak, and that water was gradually filling the cellar. Of course, we were all sent home for a couple of days off, much to the disappointment of staff and children alike, as you can imagine! It was not possible to close up the sections any further, and finding spares was proving difficult, if not impossible, so our days lengthened to a week. A replacement boiler was eventually located in some far-flung corner of the empire, and hastily dispatched in our direction. This did get as far as Cambridge, I believe, then met with the Suffolk snow and ended up in a ditch somewhere in the countryside. Our disappointment knew no bounds, another week off school!

Well, we did eventually get back after almost three weeks off, but the story didn't quite end there. There is of course a statutory number of days a school must operate. To this end some days are held in reserve for allocation by the Governors, some more by the Local Authority and even more, in real emergency by the Minister of Education. It was realised that the whole County were in excess of allocation, and it would be necessary for our school to forfeit some of our Easter Holiday!

Alan Haigh

THE PLAYGROUND

Lots of activities went on in the playground, which was a sloping one which was to the advantage of the Haverhill school when the teams came to play us. We were far better than them as they weren't used to our type of sloping playground.

We used to play in the back playground, the older ones, but the younger ones very often used to play in the front playground. The roads weren't dangerous, not when we were little, and there used to be a fountain in the middle of the junction there.

Playground Games 1916 *Jean & Bob Pavely*

When we were kids it was all big trees out the front there. And of course all the iron railings around it.

Gladys Ely

The playground sloped quite heavily, because where it's situated it begins to go up the hill to go out of the town towards Bury, up Wratting Road there. It's not like that anymore, unless it's because I was young and it seemed bigger than it was. It really sloped up at quite an angle. We always had slides in there in the winter. It was very dangerous, really, but they didn't try to stop you doing things as much as they do nowadays. I don't think they were quite as concerned for our safety as they are now. I think they thought that was all part of growing up, which I think so too really.

Christine Hart

In icy weather it was wonderful because the children would make these wonderful slides, being on the slope it was ideal for that. The caretaker would go round with his ash and cinders to make safe paths for people to walk, otherwise they would zoom down. That was one of the highlights of the winter, everybody was quite sad when it all thawed.

Hazel Smith

I can remember being thoroughly frightened by slides that went all the way down the playground. The Wratting Road end was the highest and the playground sloped down to the outside toilets, and you used to end up almost past the toilets into the little bit

where the stoke hole was, some of them. I've never seen anything so frightening in my life, absolutely lethal. But the boys used to love them, didn't they?
I used to have to walk all the way round, because from Wratting Road I could nip in the back way. But I daren't do it when those slides were on. I had to go round the front.

Jean Pavely

Pupils in Playground 1977 *History Group*

We used to make slides in the playground. We used to be forbidden really, but the boys did it mostly. They were quite lethal, I think. They looked like glass, they were absolutely lethal. And they used to be there for weeks because it just used to snow and freeze and snow and freeze. It used to be great fun on these slides. I think the boys got more fun out of it than the girls did. The girls didn't hardly dare do it.

Hilary Filben

I used to have problems sometimes getting to the school on a frosty morning, coming across an icy playground. On occasions when we had bare winters, I used to have to clear paths in all directions to get to the classes and put salt down and all that sort of thing. Sometimes just before school was going to start, down would come the snow again and undo what I'd done.
I used to go down there quite early in the morning, about half past six, clearing the playgrounds. I even used to clear outside the school, the path that runs round it because there used to be a lot of leaves come down in the playground and that was the big problem getting rid of all those. It was quite a rambling school and it involved quite a lot of work keeping it up to a standard but it always looked nice.

Albert Wade

I can always remember the big conker trees at the front where we used to throw sticks and get conkers down and get told off for doing that. There were two main ones when I was there and they were really massive. And we did our rubbings on those trees, where you put a piece of paper there and you rub it over with a crayon.

The back playground was all concrete. Only little things were done there like your bat and balls or your ball games against the walls. I remember they had painted things on the walls, a bit like hopscotch on the floor where you've got the squares where you do your hopscotch, which they had as well. You'd have to throw these balls from certain distances and you'd add up the numbers that you'd got.

Jane Duffy

In the infants, we had the conker tree and we played conkers. We also played aeroplanes where you stick your arms out. And of course I remember Rock Around The Clock around the conker tree.

Peter Isaacs

I remember there used to be a cannon. In the school just as you turned the corner there was an old First World War gun. I don't know what happened to it. They must have come and taken it away before the Second World War.

Harold Sozer

A German field gun stood in that corner, from the First World War. It stood facing up to the town. They cut it up and took it away in the Second World War for munitions. They needed the metal.

Cyril Nunn

PLAYGROUND GAMES

My best memories include playing games in the playground. Skipping games and ball games, mainly. It was always segregated really, it wasn't actually segregated in class, we segregated ourselves when we got into the playground. The girls played with the girls and the boys played with the boys. Although we played kiss chase sometimes, but normally we didn't play in mixed groups at all.

Christine Hart

Netball, rounders, mainly those activities. I think thc boys possibly played football and cricket, but the girls was mainly the netball team and the rounders because we had skipping and things like that.

Gladys Ely

Another of the games in the playground was where you'd run around and children would tag onto the end and you'd spin until someone fell off and probably break their arm.

Julie Smith

We used to play rounders a lot in the playground. I remember hitting the ball in rounders, we used to bat against what was a big corrugated building which was the carpentry shed and the balls would be pitched up towards this corrugated place. I remember I hit a ball once there and sent it clean over the school and over the main road as well. We never did find the ball after that. We had lots of games we played there, but mainly ball games and usually most of them were supervised. There'd be the odd window that got broken with a football and that sort of thing, but you didn't play football in the playground. You could throw balls about and you were allowed to play rounders.

Derek Bacon

In the back playground they used to play with balls etc. and after school, one of my main jobs was, in the back of the school there was a lot of flat roofs, I used to spend a lot of quite a bit of time after they came out getting the ladder and going up on the roof and recovering the balls.

Albert Wade

We used to play marbles, hopscotch, skipping, spinning the top, we had a top and a whip, we used to have something with stones, five stones. We didn't have the expensive toys and games that they have now. We had to do our own thing, really. I suppose I belong to the old school and I think children have too much now and they don't get the happiness out of it that we did, I don't think. I suppose we're to blame for it, we started it that way, didn't we?

Beryl Wade

It was a very big asphalt covered playground. We used to play something called shinty with some sticks, like hockey sticks. It was with a hard ball and we just knocked this around, similar to hockey. This was just the boys played that, it wasn't a mixed sort of sport.

Val Gagen

We used to have a big skipping rope where we all used to join in. It was a huge one and we all used to jump in and when you're in you're out and this sort of thing. We used to do a curving wall, a line used to curve a wall, on-hand Susie and running and that sort of thing. The boys used to play cricket in the ground and football, the usual. Rounders we used to play, touch, normal children's games. But skipping I can remember.

Gwen Salmon

Salt, mustard, vinegar, pepper, yes. I can't remember very many of those skipping rhymes. Like all kids I suppose we made up a lot of our own.

Gladys Ely

I can remember doing PE in the playground. We played a game called skittles and the other class was always better than us, we never won that. It was a bit of basically skittles with a ball, but rounders as well. Instead of your bat and ball, you had your ball and your skittles. I remember them being set up, and when you threw it you just had to run but I can't remember how many bases they had or anything like that. But it was called skittles.

Jane Duffy

We mostly just run about. Sometimes there was a fight, but that was it.

Cyril Nunn

We would skip through hoops, and put them around our waists like hoola hoops. Hopscotch was the game that was played the most, and we played this everywhere, and we were always drawing hopscotch on the roads. It was a cheap game as there was plenty of chalk around and then you only needed stones. Leapfrog was another thing, because I was always into games as we called them. I was very athletic as such, and I was always doing handstands, walking on my hands and cartwheels. When we had team games we used to have to walk up to the games field up Ratting Road. There was no grassed area, it was hard area at the school, no garden, just plain bare.

Diane Basham

I remember we used to dance in our break time in the playground. I used to dance with Gwenny Beavis, she used to have those long ringlets.

Muriel Moore

Little boys used to see if they could tiddle over the top of the outside toilet and Mr Shelley used to run in and tell them off.
There were all sorts of games; there was hopscotch and shinty. And there were these sort of clapping games.

Jean Pavely

We used to play Chinks, which I think is Five Stones or something now. I remember one incident when we were in the playground playing Chinks. These boys were playing behind me and they must have fallen on top of me because I fell and I banged my face on the playground and I broke my nose. That's why it's a funny shape now. It was bleeding everywhere and they took me to the First Aid room and they sent for my mother and what not. It put it all out of shape. I didn't have anything done to it and it's still like that now.
We used to play hopscotch and we used to swap things a lot. All the girls collected beads and we had tins of beads and swapped them. I think the boys had football cards and that sort of thing. We used to do quite a lot of that. And we used to play chase or sit around in your own little groups.

Hilary Filben

We used to watch the traffic go by because we were right on the road. We didn't worry about carbon monoxide poisoning in those days, I suppose. It was quite a big playground really, when you were little. It was always very noisy.

Karen Clark

We played some stupid games in the playground. Kiss chase of course. But I was always fairly dim because I used to run too fast and nobody would ever catch me. Well, that's my story anyway. I can remember some of the boys would play Dactari with Clarence the Cross-eyed Lion. They also did Star Trek but they were a little

group unto their own. We used to hang upside down on the bars and things.
At playtime when the whistle went, you had to stand still and then you would line up in your classes.

Jane Farrow

We played kiss cuddle and torture, or kiss cuddle and snog for the advanced. It was a game like catch but when you caught someone you offered them kiss cuddle and torture to get free and then off you'd go free again. We used to play that in the playground.
They had printed on the playground hopscotch and that type of thing. There'd be ball games. Children had just started this French Skipping, with elastic, where you had two people, one at either end. There was also a big, long skipping rope.
I remember going back to the Cangle with my husband one evening, visiting and we had a poke around in the playground. I think we'd just been to a party, we were about 19, we had a walk around because you could just walk in the back. We were reminiscing how we used to play in the playground. That was about 10 years after we'd left. I remember we went to look at the outside toilets and they seemed so tiny then.

Julie Smith

THE LESSONS

I'm very proud of my report, it's absolutely stupendous. It says, "Arithmetic very good, Reading excellent, Spelling excellent, Handwriting very good, Composition very good". I'm ever so proud of it, I never had so good a report as that again. It says, "Christine has made excellent progress this year. She is an intelligent girl who works hard. She should do very well at the high school." I was aged 10 years and 7 months at that time. I'd been at the school 6 years then, because I started in 1950.

Christine Hart

The Kedington school didn't have much at all. But Haverhill had more subjects like geometry, elementary science, art which was very good, very good sports facilities. They taught me to swim at 11 which I thought was brilliant. We seemed to settle in very well there.

I suppose 35, something like that in a class, because you had the 'A' stream, the 'B' stream and some of the lessons were amalgamated, like music, games, science, but certainly things like geometry were merged together.

I think history and art were my favourites, because I was good at art and I was always very interested in history. I was interested in music as well. I detested the singing lessons there but it's only after that when you play pieces by Schubert and Grieg and things that like that you realise that you sang those at school. The singing lessons were quite disastrous really because we would do anything we could to get out of them. We'd make out we'd got broken voices or something like that. Charlie Cotton, he was another master who used to take singing and he never really got a grip of the class. There was never a scene but it was never terribly organised. It was pleasant I suppose in some ways. Pieces like "The Trout", I remember all those pieces well. When I hear them now, I often think that they really did try at school to knock something into us, which was good.

I was always very keen on history. I was reasonable at the other subjects. I wasn't brilliant at maths, but pretty fair, sufficient to get by.

Derek Bacon

I think history and geography were my favourites. I was pretty awful at maths, I hated that. They taught maths at the blackboard with the normal books.

These days they seem to learn an awful lot from computers and so forth. I wish I'd had computers at my school, I should like to learn about them.

Val Gagen

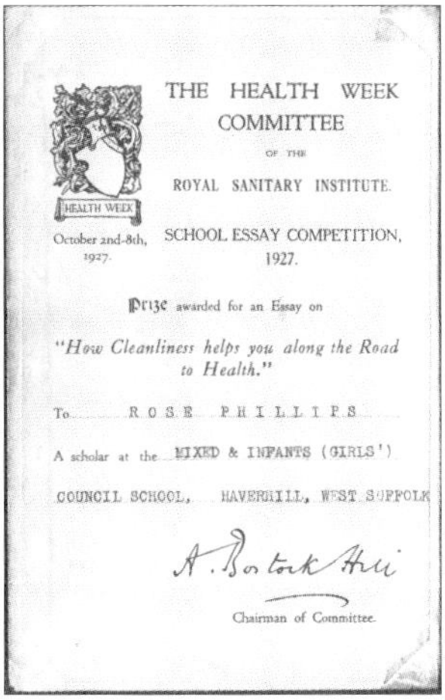
THE HEALTH WEEK
COMMITTEE
OF THE
ROYAL SANITARY INSTITUTE.

HEALTH WEEK

October 2nd-8th,
1927.

SCHOOL ESSAY COMPETITION,
1927.

Prize awarded for an Essay on

"How Cleanliness helps you along the Road to Health."

To ROSE PHILLIPS

A scholar at the MIXED & INFANTS (GIRLS')

COUNCIL SCHOOL, HAVERHILL, WEST SUFFOLK

A. Bostock Hill

Chairman of Committee.

A page from cookbook awarded to Rose Phillips

We used to do needlework, and had different teachers for different things. We did art, a lot of painting and drawing and that type of thing. My favourite was English.

Rose Philips

My favourite lessons were arithmetic and spelling and reading. I didn't like all the history stuff. On the year that I was leaving school they were teaching us algebra, I couldn't get on with that.
Our desks were wooden, and four of you could sit at each desk, and the inkpots were in the top, and little ledge where you put your pen. One child was detailed everyday to fill up the inkpots from a larger pot, which was on the mantelpiece.
One Friday one of the boys in the class was detailed to fill the inkpots, and he didn't like one of the other boys in the class. When he came to give some ink to the boy he didn't like, the boy had his head down, so he tipped the ink down his back.

Percy Sizer

It was different routines every day. Perhaps you'd have reading, arithmetic, spelling, all the different sort of subjects which you took at school. When you were in that class you stopped there and you did all your programme. Once you were in that classroom you were in there.
I took an interest in all of it; reading, writing, spelling, arithmetic. We went into all the sports and everything. We had the old-fashioned inkwells where you had to dip your ink in there. We used to do all different types of writing. We used to have learn all fancy writing. We used to do copperplate, old English etc, different styles.
We had drawing and painting. But it was mostly what they call the three 'R's. We did all the times tables, we used to go right up to twelves. One class used to take algebra, with Archie Smith. Another class, an advanced lot, they'd do shorthand and that.

Harold Sozer

I can remember the maths more because I liked maths, but I don't remember the English, and I didn't like English. We had to recite the tables, and they were drummed into you, but having said that, it was wonderful because even people who weren't very good at maths knew their tables. We had assembly and I can remember the singing because again I like singing.

Diane Basham

Girls PT in playground (Woodwork room at rear c1920) *History Group*

One of my best subjects was netball. I was good at netball and it was nice because we used to play other schools and we used to go out. I think it just used to be a chance to get out of the classroom and visit other schools. We used to wear navy blue knickers and a white T-shirt, white plimsolls and, I think, long navy socks.

Hilary Filben

I don't remember any particular favourite lessons. I remember ones that I disliked. We were going to put on a school play, or a class play, and I hated to act and I was off sick because I didn't want to act. I think it was the first, and the last, time I ever feigned an illness. I just couldn't bear the thought of standing in front of anyone.

Julie Smith

I'm into History as I'm getting older. I read actual history books. History is the subject that I have become interested in since I left school. Perhaps when you're there, you are just learning aren't you, unless you go on to do other things you don't specialise at an ordinary school. It's only now that they take options.
I was terrible at singing, but I liked dancing, netball and maths. According to my report I was top of the class in maths, so I got quite a few marks out a hundred.

Muriel Moore

We did lots of textiles with Mrs Salmon and Mrs Smith. We made peg dolls, I remember that distinctly. I can also remember a girl in my year called Susan Insole who was the most exquisite artist. She was absolutely brilliant. She'd draw the most beautiful animals. I can remember her knitting with pins and cotton and she would knit on little tiny pins.

Jane Farrow

I've always liked making things and I've always liked drawing pictures and I liked nature and growing things so I liked all the practical things, where you can do things with your hands, those were the things I enjoyed the most and I still do, even now, when I'm grown up. We used to have science lessons where we used to grow plants and things like that and we used to go for nature study walks, which I used to like and I used to like painting and drawing, and I was very keen on taking photographs when I was little and I took some photographs of the school football team once and I remember the headmaster put this photograph in a frame and put it up in his office and I was very, very proud that he had my photograph hanging up in his office.

Geoffrey Ship

MATHS

We used to have a glamourous teacher called Mr Norman, all the girls went crackers over him. He got called up unfortunately but he used to take us for Maths. We did Algebra and things like that in those days but it was all done by blackboard and chalk and our books of course. We had books which we used to have to so our sums in, for the want of a better word.
Mr Norman used to give us the Air Force entrance papers to do, the Maths on those. I can remember doing those quite vividly.

Gladys Ely

We used to sit and recite tables and I know all my tables. My son has said that he was never taught like that and my daughter wasn't either and they both consider it a great handicap that they don't know their tables. We had desks with inkwells and we sat in rows facing the front. I really don't think it did us any harm at all. Half the class passed the 11+ and went to the grammar school and the other half went to the secondary modern which was more technical. It was like vocational training and that sort of thing. I don't think there's anybody that went school when I did that doesn't know their tables. That's what I do now, work in accounts. I wasn't that good at maths, and it isn't what I really wanted to do but I can do it because I know my tables. The learning of maths like that is a thing that you just don't lose. That's the way we were taught algebra as well when I went to the grammar school. We used to sit and recite theorems all in the class. At the time we used to think, God how boring, but we've remembered it.
It's just astonishing how much things have changed in the last few years when they had been so much the same for so long. From the '60's education is virtually unrecognisable now.

Christine Hart

We used to have, which was my real favourite, mental exams, where you had 10 questions and you had to write the answers down. I did like that. We didn't have a lot of apparatus and things or visual aids. We did it all with a pen and pencil and paper, apart from the slates. We learned adding up, subtraction, multiplication and division. We didn't do much in the way of percentages and things until we were a bit older.

Beryl Wade

Maths was taught in the traditional way, you had all the normal things, the tables, the algebra, the problems. We didn't have all these logarithms and things like that, it was algebra, multiplication, division, pounds, shillings and pence, weights and measures, really basic maths in those days. It was quite useful and I still think it is. It beats me how people can work and yet they don't know their tables, because that was instilled into us. That was our first lesson on maths, mental arithmetic. We had to know our tables and anything the teacher used to dot about and ask us at random different tables; four sixes, eight nines and this sort of thing. And if you didn't know it, then you lost a house point so it was very important to us as kids to know our tables. We used to do that and the 'avoir du poids' I think they used to call the weight table, we had to learn that. And feet and inches. And you never forget them. I don't forget them now, I can remember them because you used to chant them so much that it really went in, which my grandchildren are just starting to do. I think it's a very good idea.

Gwen Salmon

I have been retired for several years now, and I actually think we've come full cycle. Youngsters were expected to know their tables and things like that. We still had the 11+ when I first came here. We were streamed, but they knew their tables and we had spelling tests, so I don't think it was that different really. I think we've been through a phase of things being different, but children all sat at desks in twos and faced the teacher and the blackboard, which they're beginning to do again.

Hazel Smith

I can remember chanting endlessly times tables. You used to have to learn a new one every now and again. The whole class used to chant that times table. With the whole class chanting it, you weren't perceived to make a mistake and a fool of yourself in the same way as if one child was asked to do it alone. But that was drummed in. I know that that's considered wrong to drum things into children now, but it lasts a lifetime.

Jean Pavely

I wasn't very good at Maths, I didn't like Maths very much. We had to learn our tables. We'd sail through the easy ones, like the 2's and the 5's and the 10's, but when it came to the 9's and the 7's it was a bit more difficult. But you had to learn your tables. We had three groups for Maths; A, B and C. I was in C, I'm afraid, but I kept fairly near the top of C so it wasn't too bad. We did all the addition and subtraction, not maths like it is now. It seems quite terrifying now, some of the maths. But then, it was just the main: addition, subtraction, multiplication, division etc. It wasn't one of my best subjects, I'm afraid.

Hilary Filben

I can remember mental arithmetic, decimal points and fractions, which I just love. I still like a challenge now with figures.

Muriel Moore

Maths was mostly illustrated on the blackboard. You had your textbooks and the system was always described and illustrated on the blackboard. Multiplication tables were taught parrot-fashion, and I have to say I still remember them. It was one of the first things I was taught and that's one of the few things I really remembered. It's been very useful. Maths was never my brilliant subject, but I do remember mental arithmetic which can help you get by most things.

Tony Stevens

I can remember a teacher called Miss Smith, it was a double-barrelled name but it was Miss Smith and she played the piano. We had Maths with her. I don't think I was particularly brilliant at Maths. I can remember a theme of time and we had to do all these things to do with time. I got really upset and blared my eyes out because I couldn't tell the time and I found it really difficult. I must have been about nine, and I really struggled with this and got quite upset. She was very comforting and reassuring. We must have got through it somehow because I'm quite good now.

Jane Farrow

ENGLISH

English was always my favourite subject at school. I started to read quite early on and I've always liked reading and drama. We didn't really do very much in the way of school plays, not when I was at school then. I used to write about what I did on my holidays, what I wanted to be when I grow up.

Christine Hart

We did the ordinary traditional alphabet in those days. It was done by sounding out of the vowels and the consonants and building them up and recognising them. We had pictures and you recognised them by things like that.

Beryl Wade

I was a very bad speller and I used to like writing stories, but the writing was atrocious. But my heart went into it and that was another thing Miss Gilbert spotted. She'd put out the right words and gave me plenty to time to write it out again and then get me to read it in front of the class because she liked my stories.

Peter Isaacs

We wrote with pens and ink. We had a little inkpot in the desk, one of these where you dip in. Every so often someone would put their hand up and say, "Please can I have a new nib?". You used to slide the nib in to write with. It wasn't really messy, depending on what you did. If you just dobbed it in and pulled it out there'd be a big blotch all over everywhere. But if you took care, it wasn't messy.

Cyril Nunn

When I started at the school, they wouldn't let me write in looped writing as I had been taught. I had to learn to write again missing out all the loops, and I always think that ruined my handwriting. I can remember the inkwells, one in each desk, always for a right-handed child.

Jean Pavely

You can see that my writing has no loops, and I have never been allowed to do loops. When we go to high school, the girls from the other side of Sudbury used loops. Once you have got to 11 your style is already formed. They must have done loops in the older days because my father had lovely writing. All my family had lovely flowing writing with loops on. My mother, who went to the same school as my father, had the most peculiar writing and it wasn't actually joined. It was all separate letters all the way along, and she was two years younger and perhaps had a different teacher.

Diane Basham

We had a big stone bottle of ink and you'd go and tip them in there, ink used to go all over everywhere. Your fingers and that used to be all ink.

Bob Pavely

My favourite subject was English. We used to have to write compositions. I did like writing compositions and I think I must have been quite good at them because the teacher very often used to read mine out in front of the class. There's only one thing, I tended to go on and on and on and not stop when I should have done.
My spelling wasn't too bad. They really were very strict on spelling years ago. You had spelling tests and everything, which I think they do again now. I think they did go through a time when teachers thought spelling wasn't that important, as long as the children got the work down, it didn't matter how it was spelt. It wasn't like that when I went to school. We had spelling tests and we had to get the spellings right.

Hilary Filben

The least favourite thing for me was writing anything. My writing was absolutely appaling then. You can read my writing now, but at that time it was very hard to read. I quite liked English then, despite my writing. I enjoyed it a bit more than the rest.

Gerry Kiernan

WOODWORK

There was big tin shed which belonged to Hovis and we had a carpentry class. I made a cabinet. Mr Savoury the teacher was, the head carpenter.

Ted Basham

We had a playground at the back of the school. Where you've got the new houses built on there now, that used to be a carpenter's shop up there. You had to learn how to make dovetail joints and all sorts of things like that. If you didn't take notice, you'd get a bit of wood or a mallet thrown at you. Mr Savoury was the teacher. We used to make pipe racks and knife boxes and things like that.

Harold Sozer

At the top end of the playground was the carpentry shed. Savoury, he was the carpentry teacher. We used to go up there and make dovetail joints and stools and things like that; little toolboxes where you'd put screwdrivers and that in to carry about, with handles.

Cyril Nunn

NEEDLEWORK

Needlework Class *Mrs Iron*

Mrs Beer used to teach us our sewing and how to make things and particularly smocking. I can remember that vividly as it was the only thing I was good at, because I'm not very friendly with a needle. I don't like sewing, but I did like embroidery and smocking. We didn't have machines in those days, it was all hand sewing, everything you made was hand made.
I don't think girls did woodwork in those days. Girls were left to the girly things, boys did woodwork and metalwork.

Gladys Ely

I think we only went about one day to needlework because a lot of us didn't like that teacher. We used to have to keep one piece of tacking cotton and keep using it over and over again. That teacher's name was Miss Gent.
We had one sewing machine there, which was hand operated and we used to take it in turns. We were all girls. The boys did woodwork.

Rose Philips

ART

We did paintings, we called it painting, it wasn't called art. We didn't have an art room; when you were in a particular class you tended to do most of your lessons in that class. There weren't very many rooms that were actually for a specific purpose.

Christine Hart

Art was one of my best subjects. We did a lot of drawing and painting and with the war on, we did posters for War Weapons Week and that sort of thing. I can't remember in detail now, but I know there was a lot of pencil drawing.

Derek Bacon

I liked doing pictures at the Cangle. I still do it as a hobby. At the Cangle we used blobby, watercolour things with big, thick brushes. I wasn't brilliant, but I can remember people like Mrs Shelley and other teachers praised me for it. I think it was because they did look a bit like what I was supposed to be painting.

Peter Isaacs

I liked art. It was probably one of my favourite lessons. I used to especially like it when we used to go out with a drawing board. We used to go round the town and into the fields and draw things, buildings and still life etc. The art room was separate as well from the main school; it was a prefab building in the playground. We had tubes of paint that you mixed up with water and they were all kept in the art cupboard. When the class started, we were allowed to get a tube and have one little blob of each colour and that was it. We had to make that last, we weren't allowed any more. So if you put too much water on your brush you had very pale, watery colours. And we used to do pictures with chalks and pastels. Mr McGregor, he was the art teacher and was quite strict. You could relax and talk, you didn't have to study too hard. The best pictures used to be put round the classroom. I think I might have had one or two put round while I was there. We had craft too. We used to cover our books and learn how to do the corners properly. We used to make folders and little mats. I quite enjoyed that as well. We had needlework too. A lot of the things we made we could use at school. But we also made things for our mothers and fathers, things to take home. I've probably still got some of them kicking around now somewhere.

Hilary Filben

One of the other classrooms I can remember was pottery, again for some bizarre reason. I don't remember the English or the Maths, they must have been really uninteresting. But I can remember the pottery because that was in the block at the back, the prefabs next to what was the dining area, and throwing the clay on and making a mess of it.

Karen Clark

SWIMMING

We did sport, but the only thing I was any good at was netball because I was tall and I was shooter. I couldn't run, but I did swim, we used to go swimming. We used to go up the waterworks but while I was at Cangle there was a swimming pool across which is now opposite what used to be the old police station but is now Archers building. We used to have a gala and I was a little girls champion. We did life saving as well. The prizes were little medals. I think we had things like little pencil sets. We used to have to take the chairs from the school down to the swimming bath, go in line and I can remember taking my chair and all walking down in line, but it was only across the road.

Beryl Wade

Swimming Pool 1931 *History Group*

We went swimming and I can remember my mum because they used to ask parents to come with us occasionally so there was always so many adults per children. I can remember feeling very poorly because I had a reaction to swimming. I still do slightly now. It must be the chlorine in the water. It used to make me either sick or bring my skin out very puffy and all my eyes. It wasn't connected until a couple of years afterwards because sometimes it wasn't very aggressive so it would be like a bit of itchy eye. But sometimes it was very aggressive and it would come up. I can't remember if it was once a week or once every two weeks but I do definitely remember going swimming.

Jane Duffy

We did swimming, and we had an old swimming bath up Burton End, and we used to have to walk up there. I never learned to swim.

Rose Philips

Well, the swimming pool was only just a short walk from the school, along the Pikeall. It was an open-air pool, and there was just a foot bath to go through, not a shower, to get to the cubicles. It was not heated and there were diving boards. The temperature was always up on the side, and when it was 59 degrees it was pretty cold. We must have been taken there and learned to swim there because I remember having a blown-up rubber ring put around me and ropes. I can see somebody now, pulling me towards the side so I'd got my feet off of the ground. Initially we learned to do breaststroke because I never liked putting my face in the water, and we didn't learn to dive. I used to have a season ticket and I can remember spending everyday in the summer holidays and after school, when it was fine, down at the swimming pool.

Diane Basham

MUSIC

We did have music lessons in which we sat round the piano and had to sing songs "Oh for the wings of a dove" or things like that, but Mrs Highly used to take us in those days for music lessons and she used to play and we used to have hymns. There was assembly each morning, we used to have hymns and a prayer.

Gladys Ely

There was not very much music. We did have cymbals and tambourines and things like that. We were all quite young, weren't we? It was quite basic music. We were taught nursery rhymes and we had singing. One of the reasons why I know a lot of old-fashioned folk songs and things is because we used to do that at school.

Christine Hart

We had assembly every morning. It was a bit different from what they are now. Now it's not a specific religion, I don't think. But then it was a real little service really. I remember 444 was 'All things bright and beautiful'. We used to sing those sort of songs. 'Now the day is over', real hymns. It got to be Songs of Praise towards the end but they were the real church hymns.

Beryl Wade

We had assembly every day in those days, a religious assembly. They don't today, do they? We always had a hymn to start the day, that was the first thing you did, you went to assembly then you went to your class and had your register.

We used to do a lot of singing with parts, three different voices. You had to find out where your voice was and we had all this three-part singing which I used to quite like. We used to have London's Burning and I've got a bit of deep voice so I used to be down the bottom, alto I think they used to call it. We used to have to sound off our voice so she could put us where we were.

Gwen Salmon

We did music, but we didn't have musical instruments, just tambourines and triangles, if I can remember. The dragon, Mrs Gillespie, had a piano. It's funny, but I turned out musical.

I went on to play banjo, squeeze box, in fact when I was made redundant I went busking and got onto the folk circuit. I still play now, I do barn dances and concerts. But that didn't start until I was about 14.

Peter Issacs

In assembly we used to sing 'New Every Morning is the Love' and then they used to read a piece out of the Bible. One thing, which they've stopped now which is terrible, we all used to have to learn a verse out of the Bible.
"In all thy ways acknowledge Him and He will direct thy path"

Percy Sizer

Every morning, when we went in at nine o'clock the shutters were all drawn across back and that was your morning service in there. There used to be one of the preachers from the town who came in. One would take it one week and one take it another. After the service, the shutters were drawn back and you were all in your separate classes.

Harold Sozer

We always learned carols. To this day, those are the tunes that I like to sing. Miss Potter, who was the headmistress, was a musician. She used to do the assembly. She used to have the National Song Book and the Songs of Praise. In Songs of Praise, I can tell you now, that 'All Things Bright and Beautiful' is number 444. The National Song Book meant that you had to have the Harp that once in Tara's Halls for the Irish, and then you had to learn Land of My Fathers for the Welsh. We never did learn anything for the English, I'm sure we didn't. They all seemed to have their national songs which we had to learn, but not the English ones. Strawberry Fair, I suppose. But she used to love that National Song Book and she used to consider that that was part of her duty that we learned what you might call fairly decent music to sing.

Jean Pavely

One of the lessons that has always stuck out, and it's a disjointed, obscure memory actually, is the music lessons. I'm not musically orientated in any way, but I always remember there was a three-storey block on the left hand side of the back playground. The music teacher, I can't remember her name, but she was quite tall and slim and she had quite red hair. I remember she went to Kenya for a holiday and she brought back various African instruments and artefacts and things and that was really interesting. A lot of drumming went on for quite some time after a while with all these African instruments.

I can always remember the music books, and this is the really bizarre memory that you have. The colouring on them was an abstract colour, they were purple and green. I don't know why the front of these books was purple and green. I'm not musically orientated, I must have just liked her as a teacher.

Karen Clark

We had a music master called Mr Kibble who was also the organist at the old independent church. He was a fanatical person for getting it right. He would make you go over and over again on these songs. He would put the descants in and he would go over and over it until he got it absolutely perfect. He had his pet ones who could sing better than the others. They used to go into singing competitions as well. I quite liked music, in fact he used to give piano lessons privately as well. Unfortunately, I was going to learn the piano but he gave me the sack after one term because I wasn't making sufficient progress. He was very strict. He was a white-haired little man, very old. He seemed to be around for years and years.

Tony Stevens

We had assembly in the main hall, where we had our dinner and where the school play was. If you were in trouble, you were called down to the front in school assembly.

Gerry Kiernan

SEX EDUCATION

We didn't have Sex Education until I'd been there a little while and then they decided to have it. I've no idea what they called it but I can remember that the boys went up to the town hall. We didn't have it in school, we had it in the town hall and we had three days in which the girls went one day, the boys went the following day and then on the third time we all were together asking questions but I can't remember who did it. I don't know if it was one of the local doctors. We never had many doctors in those days but I can remember that part of it, but having said that you were always too frightened. If you went out with a boy before you got home your parents knew it because it was one of those towns where the word got round. How it got round I don't know as we didn't have telephones in those days but I could bet your bottom dollar if I went to the Friday night youth club I used to come home from the Cangle and round the downs and if I spoke to anybody by the time I'd got home to Chainey Pieces my Auntie would say you've been talking to so and so. So you could never do anything in this town without everybody else knowing really.

Gladys Ely

We had sex education when we were 11+ and I can remember learning about it in biology from another girl sitting next to me. I said, "what is that?" and I had it explained like that.

Diane Basham

We never had sex education, it was never mentioned. I don't know whether that was a good thing or a bad thing really. Having said that, I do remember about four girls getting pregnant when they were about 15 in that time I was there. Obviously some of the girls were more forward than others. One of the prefects kept me and my friend in after class at midday We were given a very sharp bit of sex education from these two prefects who were older than us. They were both 15 year old girls and big at that. There was never anything taught about it. I think probably the girls had some education as to what happened when they had their first period I suppose, but nothing more than that I don't think.

Tony Stevens

GARDENING

Then of course we had gardening. That was quite funny. As you go along the relief road towards what is now the Co-op car park and the roundabout, somewhere around that area was where the school gardens were. The class would often go along there and those of us who lived in the villages anyway and well conversant with gardening were sometimes sent to the garden to get things sorted out a bit. This we used to do, we used to be quite interested in this but we were also very keen on swimming. En route we passed the swimming baths and I remember one day the headmaster caught us all in the swimming baths and all our implements stood against the fence. That was the last time we had to go in fact.

Derek Bacon

Up in the area of the town that's is now called Puddlebrook there used to be a Victorian building that had been the old isolation hospital. Two of the staff actually lived there, and there was quite a lot of garden attached to it, and it was the school garden. When the boys were timetabled for gardening they would traipse all the way from the Cangle up there and spent the morning, or the whole afternoon. They used to grow vegetables and it was George Hunter who was the gardening teacher, and that was his specialism. We did have, open days when the parents could go up and we had an evening in the school garden, which was quite interesting. They used to grow all these rows of lettuces and peas and things. Sometimes they would sell them or they could take them home if it was their patch.

Hazel Smith

We had a garden up Wratting Road and Archie Smith used to make us march up there. We had a little plot and we learned gardening.

Ted Basham

As you got into the top of class, you had a plot of land. It was just as you got to the top of Wratting Hill where the nurseries are. There were two of you on each plot. The produce from that, you could buy. Right at the top end of it we had three or four hives of bees. A chap used to come from Bury St Edmunds to show us how to take all the honey out. That was an afternoon's lesson. You could buy the honey.

Harold Sozer

Something else that they had then that they don't seem to have now, is they had a garden for the boys to do gardening. There were actually two gardens, or allotments. There was one along the relief road, which is so built up now but before it was the relief road there was a garden there, behind a fence, for the boys to grow vegetables and flowers and all sorts of things. Then there was another one, it's where the Chimswell is now. There was an old isolation hospital up there and the school garden used to be up there. I don't think they have gardening on the curriculum now. The girls didn't go there. I can remember going once but only to look round, we didn't actually do any gardening. We did cookery. I think now boys do cookery and girls would have done gardening. But then, it wasn't heard of for boys to do cookery, it was a girl's thing, and gardening was a boy's thing. We were kept quite separate like that.

Hilary Filben

We put the seeds in between us and we put the potatoes in, and Mr Gagen mashed all the potatoes in the hole with end of the hoe. Because of that we got the best crop of potatoes and got recommended for that. In the seedbed we only had two weeds come up.

I don't know what happened to the potatoes. There were no school dinners in those days. I suppose the teachers had them.

We used to have bees. Mr Crete used to come down, he was the school gardener. He used to take us up to look after the bees. There were only two of us went at a time, Wal Grieves and myself. We used to get a coil of cardboard and put in this blower, light it and blow it out, pump the bellows and it put a puff of smoke into the beehive. When the bees were all dopey, you take the top off and lift the frames up and pull all the dead bees out and put them back in again.

The metal flips on the end of the frames went into the combs and we used to make new clips to put on. We used to do metalwork as well, we made these clips by hand.

Robert Pavely

SCIENCE

We did do science but I wasn't very good at it, I never have been. I only did it for a couple of years when I got into the grammar school and then I had to drop it because I was just so hopeless, I just couldn't fathom it out at all, especially physics.

Christine Hart

One of the things I remember most vividly about science, although we only did elementary stuff like expansion and contraction, but I do remember very, very clearly a great big jar of mercury, someone dropping it and there were three of us. I wasn't involved in this really, but I still had to help pick all these small bubbles of mercury up which, when you think about it for hygiene, that's not terribly clever really.

Derek Bacon

There was what they called a gas cupboard in the lab. Pupils used to put their head in and have a sniff but you didn't sniff for long.

We used to have the chemicals and that in the lab and we used to have tweezers to pick the little pieces of scales, grams and that, and balance the stuff out on the scales. There was some phosphorus which they used to keep in water in a jar. Well, if that dried out a piece of phosphorus used to catch fire, so that was always kept locked up in the cupboard. We used to make some real messes with the Bunsen burner and test tubes and things. I had a chemical set myself at home. Father said we'll make some oxygen. We got it in a test tube and it all bubbled out all black and stained the scrub top table that we had in the kitchen. You couldn't get it to stain out of the kitchen table, that was there for good. I said that if that was oxygen, I don't want it.

Robert Pavely

COOKERY

The girls didn't do woodwork, the girls had cookery. That used to be above Marion Castle's schoolroom. Miss Phillips was the cookery teacher whilst I was there.

Muriel Moore

The girls baked jam tarts and mince pies, things like that. They used to come downstairs with them on a tray. We used to come out of class and, well they never used to take many home.

Bob Pavely

We had a nice cookery room, which was upstairs. Mrs Phillips was the cookery teacher. I had quite a few failures, and successes, in the cookery room. One of my failures was semolina; we didn't like that and I think my father's chickens ate it in the end. I think one of the things I did quite well was cheese and potato pie. That went down very well.

When we were in the top class, we actually spent nights there. They had a flat there and some of the girls stayed there, under supervision of course. We'd have a weekend there, or a night there and look after ourselves; do our own cookery and cleaning and learn to be housewives, I suppose. That was very good.

We used to make the teachers tea. The teachers had a staff room and it was the pupils' duty to make the tea. I remember once, I must have been quite naughty really, I put salt in the tea instead of sugar. I think it was for a dare. That didn't go down very well. I don't think I owned up to it because there was quite a few of us making tea at the time.

Hilary Filben

SPORTS

We had a sports field which is up on Wratting Road because where we were we'd only got the hard surface playground. We used to go up there and play rounders and athletics more than anything. We didn't play netball or anything like that, but it was only a primary school. I only went to the primary school. There was a secondary part of it but I didn't go to that so I don't know what sort of sports they did then. I know for sports days we were always up on that playing field up there. That's still used as a playing field. My grandsons train football on there now.

Christine Hart

Pupils (Athletics) 1966 *Newspaper cutting*

We had a very good netball team at the time when I was there and we used to go to away matches, to Brandon and places like that to play different schools.

Gladys Ely

One of my big achievements was in 1943 when I won the athletic championship. I was very keen on athletics. I won the 100 yards easily. I won the 220, with the help of a dog that was chasing me round as well. This is true as well; there was a small gap, the gap got rather bigger when the dog chased me. So I won the 220, I won the long jump, I came second in the high jump, second in throwing the cricket ball and our team, the red team, we won the relay as well. We should have had a medal but they said that as it was wartime, we'd get them after the war, but we never got one. Most of the families were there. I don't believe I told my parents that the sports were on the go.

Derek Bacon

We used to do gym. The playing fields in those days, the sports field, was at the top of Wratting Road. But we used to have to walk up there to our sports field and do all the sports up there. We used to wear navy blue knickers and a white top. If you hadn't got any of them you used to have to tuck your dress in, which was most embarrassing. I never used to like sports a lot. I used to like hockey and netball, but not running and things like that. We used to go up there once or twice a week, I suppose.

We had a nice big hall where we did our gym and we had a playground where we could do small things. But major events were always at Wratting Road. We used to have one sports day where parents could come, we used to think that was nice, but not many parents did because a lot of the men were away anyway and I suppose the women were recruited. I can't remember a big audience. I remember once we were up there and the siren went and a doodlebug was coming over. We all had to lie down on the field. It came over and the fire stopped in the tail just above us, but it landed about six or seven miles away. We thought that was great, we never thought about the danger of it, it was the excitement of seeing this doodlebug come over. But things like that you do remember.

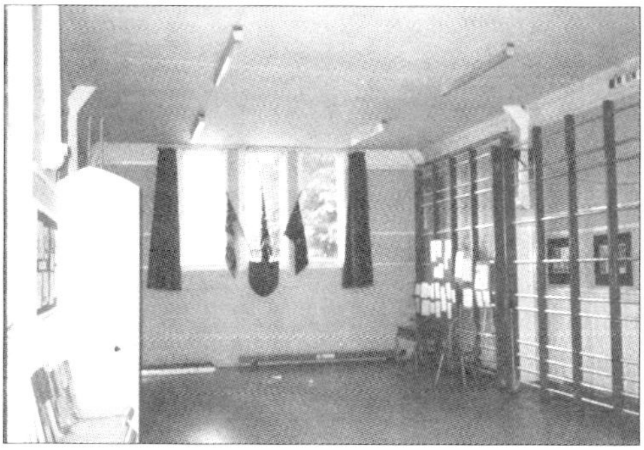

Gymnasium at front of school 1977 *History Group*

Gwen Salmon

The main sports were done on the field at the top which is actually next to Samuel Ward's Upper School. That's where we had our sports days, which I was never any good at. I never came last but I was never first either. But they used to be really good fun.

Jane Duffy

We didn't mix sexes. It was separate PE where as now they are all together. The girls did netball, rounders and athletics in the summer, which was nice up on the field, but you couldn't do much on that sloping playground. There was a small hall inside and in the winter or wet days you could in there and do certain amount of country dancing and physical activities. It was very limiting to say the least.

Hazel Smith

I wasn't a keen sportsman, that's for sure. I think we had things like skipping ropes. We did have sports day; we used to walk up Wratting Hill from the Cangle. We had sack races and things like that.

Peter Isaacs

We used to play football and cricket at Steeple Bumstead. We struck lucky there one day because there were two boys at Steeple Bumstead, they were twins and that was their birthday and we had a lovely spread.

Ted Basham

Footbal Team 1933 (including left to right)
PW Underwood (Head), BM Gurteen (School Manager) A Smith (Sportsmaster)
History Group

Father was in the parent teachers association when they had a sports day. Being a butcher, he had about the only refrigerator in the town. He said to Miss Potter when they were organising this sports day that we'd give every child an ice cream. He did it by sending the firm's van to wherever the ice cream came from, bringing it, storing it in the butcher's fridge until the last minute and then having it taken up to the school field, also in the firm's van which wasn't refrigerated in those days. He did actually get every child an ice cream on the sports field. That was considered a considerable feat in those days, to give every child an ice cream. Now you don't think much about an ice cream, apart from how much they cost.

Jean Pavely

I remember on sports days, we had to carry a little chair, in a crocodile, up the road and onto the playing field. We got all the chairs sorted out and we used to have the school sports day. All the parents used to come and sit on the little chairs. Inevitably there used to be a storm and everybody used to disperse and run for the nearest tree.
I was quite good at the long jump and the high jump because I was tall. Not so much running. We always had prizes. I don't think they have prizes now, I think they just have coloured badges. But we had prizes; books or tokens or something, for first, second and third. We wore our little strip to say what colour we were in. I did enjoy the sports days. I didn't enjoy walking up there with the chairs or walking back with the chairs afterwards.

Hilary Filben

We had a school cricket team and a school football team. I was fortunate enough to be good enough to play for the school all the time that I was there. I wasn't so good at cricket. We had active sports, with sports days and inter-school challenge events. My brother, who is a year older than me, was always quite good at cricket. On one sports day, they were having a throwing the cricket ball competition and he threw the cricket ball and the headmaster, who was standing there supervising, this cricket ball came down and hit him on the head and knocked him out cold. He didn't get into trouble, it was a pure accident. He just shouldn't have been standing there. It became a bit of a joke after that. On sports days he used to wear an ex-army tin helmet.

Tony Stevens

Football was my favourite sport. I suppose that was another big wrench for me, because I'd gone from living just near the football ground in Fulham. That season was just coming to an end and I think I'd been to every match. I'd even go to reserve matches. Then ending up in Haverhill with not a football team in sight really. It was really a few years just supporting teams, changing around a little bit but never really going to football then until I was old enough to travel.

Gerry Kiernan

Pupils (Sports) 1966 *Newspaper cutting*

I can remember Mr Roy taking us for PE and we had races. I always used to win, but I always used to beat all the boys as well. He was quite astounded at this and would mention this to my mother. We had little ribbons on sports day for first, second and third. If you came first you had a little yellow ribbon which represented gold. If you came second you had a little white one which represented silver. And if you came third you had a brown one for bronze. I think you could only go in for so many races, but if you won all five, or the person who won their most, had a little cup. I can remember one year I had five yellow ribbons and another girl called Jane had five yellow ribbons and we shared this little cup. It was probably about six inches tall and we had that for six months each. We had to go up in assembly and receive that.

There was a sports meeting between the primary schools at Place Farm. We took part and I came third in a running race and had to go and collect a certificate from Mr Hutchinson. I can remember having a sty or something hideous which was weeping, so I could barely make my way there.
We used to have our gym lessons across the road at the Corn Exchange. We used to get some apparatus out, but it was always cold over there. I don't think I liked that very much. I liked my home comforts too much.

Jane Farrow

I used to like PE. The boys and the girls used to do it. There was a knack in vaulting over the box horse. We used to do all that. You bend your head so you land on your shoulders not your head. Then we used to do pyramids. I used to be at the bottom of the pyramid, thank goodness, not way up at the top. We used to jump and somersault around like that. Look at me now! We used the hall where we used to do the singing.

Robert Pavely

DANCING

We used to have ballroom dancing as part of a lesson and in those days we used to have to go across to the old Corn Exchange which is still there now opposite and I can remember then with my daughter saying about getting the splinters. How we did ballroom dancing there I'll never know really because it was all up and down.

Gladys Ely

We used to have dancing lessons and if you didn't get a partner that was tough because everyone had to form up somehow. It used to be rather embarrassing in some ways. I didn't like dancing then. I did manage to learn to dance, under protest, and afterwards I got quite involved after I left school.

Derek Bacon

We had country dancing and that was really funny because one week it would be the girls had to pick the boys and then the second week it would be the boys would have to pick the girls. I can remember it just being an awful time. You could look at the boys and they were so embarrassed. I used to go running up to one and just grab them and say, "You're being my partner". They had no choice.

Jane Duffy

We had folk dancing, Miss Castle took that; Circassian Circle and Dargassan, that was in the hall. We used to have music in there with Miss Gowers.

Muriel Moore

The girls loved country dancing but all the boys hated it. They had to do it and some of them really hated it. It was really nice, we enjoyed it. We used to have an after school club country dancing, but that was mainly girls dancing with girls because the boys didn't have to come so they wouldn't, you'd only get one or two. I used to enjoy that.

Hilary Filben

HISTORY

I think History is always interesting, because if you don't know where you came from, how do you know what you're like or who you are? I think history's very important because you need to learn about the way people lived before and maybe if they made mistakes you can avoid them then. And if they had good things to teach you then you should be able to learn from them.
The lessons of history need to be learned because a lot of the trouble that there is in the world is because people are not interested in how other people live or how they have lived and they don't want to see their points of view. I think it's important that you do. History can teach you a lot of that. You can understand why people are they way they are and then it makes you more tolerant of them.

Christine Hart

I used to like history, I had a good teacher - Miss Gilbert I think. She suffered from epilepsy. She'd read a book to the class and talk about the Romans. I wasn't an academic in any way really. I was very much behind. It wasn't until later I caught up.

Peter Isaacs

FRENCH

I couldn't get on with French very well. I suppose it's because I didn't pay enough attention really. We had a good French teacher, but language was very new then in schools. We were lucky enough to have it, I suppose, but I don't think any of us really took it that seriously. The poor teacher, she was French, I think she used to despair with us. I think we had her in tears so many times, it's awful when you think of it now. Mrs Hazel her name was. I don't think we were really interested in it, it's not like it is now. You can make use of French so much now, but in those days it was such a foreign language and we probably wouldn't need it anyway. I don't think she got much of a response from the class. I don't think anyone had been to France. People didn't go abroad much then, did they? You went to the seaside here and that.

Hilary Filben

EXAMINATIONS

I think we had an exam about Easter time. But then we had the main exam just before the summer holidays. That's when we used to get our school reports. I always knew what mine was going to say. You get in with a group with the same mind as yourself. We used to get on with our work but also we used to talk a lot and have fun. It doesn't seem to me as if people took it quite as seriously as they do now. There was the 11+ and if you passed that you were clever. I didn't pass it and my brother didn't pass it either. My brother was at school with me, he was in the year below me. My sister passed, so she must have been the clever one of the family, and then she went on to Sudbury on the bus. They stopped the 11+ soon after that anyway.
There was quite a divide between the grammar school children in Haverhill and the ones that carried on at the Cangle. If they passed the 11+ they were considered really clever. They were looked up to because they went off to grammar school in Sudbury. I quite liked the fact that I could stay in Haverhill and walk to school. We had quite a few after school clubs that we went to. I wouldn't have minded going on the bus. I was always rather envious of them because they all had school uniform and they all looked so smart. They all used to stand there and I always used to think that they looked down on us a bit because they were going to grammar school.

Hilary Filben

Another memory was actually doing my 11+. I hadn't done the 11+ because we didn't have the 11+ in London. I hadn't been there very long and everyone else had done it.

West End Church school room (overspill)
History Group

There was myself and one other who I knew was in the same year and he'd been away for a while and had come back, so he'd missed a lot as well.
We were both set up into one of these upstairs classrooms above the head teacher's office, I think, somewhere like that, which was near the middle entrance at the front. We were put in this tiny little room and given this test. I'm not exactly sure we knew it was the 11+. I think it was all a bit vague as to what it was at the time because we were just sort of dragged in to do it. And we both failed it. But we were given the afternoon off so we went and played football for a while and generally dossed around the town.
He's the one person now who I still have contact with, Andrew Rollinson. Failing the 11+ didn't do

him any harm really, because he's now one of Tesco's senior managers over a region, so he seems to be doing alright for himself. I still see him at least a few games a season of football now in Cambridge, so we still meet him. It's my one lasting contact from Cangle.

Gerry Kiernan

We took an exam called the 11 plus and most of my friends passed the 11 plus and I did as well, and then if you passed this exam you went to another school in Sudbury called a grammar school and if you didn't pass this exam you went to a school in Haverhill called the secondary modern school which is now Castle Manor School and I really wanted to go there, but the only reason I really went to the grammar school is that lots of my friends passed the exam as well, so I was quite sad to leave here and in some ways I wished I could have gone to the other school because I liked doing lots of things with my hands like making things and art and craft things and you didn't do very much of that at the school I went to.

Geoffrey Ship

Annie Buttle's Certificate of Merit from 1904 *Mr Laver*

THE TEACHERS

I always thought that it was a very happy school with nice teachers and some of them lived locally then in those days. I think they belonged to various groups and things that were in the town. So I think the staff then did seem to associate more with the town than they do now.

Gladys Ely

I remember the headmistress very well. Her name was Miss Potter. She was a very tall woman it seemed to me at the time. She was very like the headmistress that Alistair Sim plays in The Happiest Days of your Life. She took us for needlework as well as being the headmistress. I remember Mr Carr, he only died a few years ago. His name's Reginald Carr and we used to be streamed as we got older, from about 8 or 9, and if you were in the top part of his class you sat at the right hand side in the rows and that was called the "creamy top". There was another teacher there called Mr Lay who was incredibly handsome. He looked like Gregory Peck. We were all in love with him when we were about seven. Then there was Mrs Corkindale and she took the top class. She's the one who wrote that glowing report for me, because she was my last teacher there. I think the name of the one I disliked so much was Mrs Scott. She was a short, fat woman with glasses and she was absolutely horrible. I wonder what happened to her, something awful I hope!

Christine Hart

Miss Castle was my first teacher. They put us in the 'A' stream and I went to 2A, Miss Castle's class and then from there to 3A, Mr Williams. Other teachers were Archie Smith who was a reporter for The Echo and he was fanatical about sport. If you were good at sports you'd get on with Archie no trouble at all.
Archie was the type of person who would trick boys. In geometry, if he saw someone struggling a bit he'd draw a large circle and a small circle and he'd say, "Now, boy, how many degrees are there in this circle" and the boy would look, I suppose, and someone would whisper something to him and then for the next one, much smaller, "Oh, about 75 in that one". Quite a lot of trouble developed from that sort of thing. It wasn't really fair. I think he thought it was funny but when you think about it now, it wasn't really funny at all. But if you were reasonable at sport then everything was fine.

Derek Bacon

As an infant there, all the teachers seemed very elderly. It was very strict. We wrote on slates. When my husband was caretaking he went up in the attic and he found all the old slates that we used to write on. We used to have to sit in class and not talk and the teacher stood at the front. They'd all got their own peculiarities. There was Minnie Mason, she was the arithmetic teacher. It was called arithmetic in those days, nothing else just arithmetic. That was one of my favourite subjects. She had a wonderful habit of having a pencil and clicking you on the knuckles. That was her punishment. There was Miss Lilly Callow, I think she was history and geography if I remember properly. There was a Miss Annie Gowers who lived up Broad Street. She must have been English and Drama because she introduced me to Shakespeare who I really liked. We had quite a big outing. She took four of her, I suppose we were favourites, up to London to see a Shakespeare play, that was the highlight of the year. There was Marian Castle, she came in as a young student and she did PE etc. The headmistress Annie Webb. It really was just a girls school, the girls and the boys were divided, we weren't mixed. We had a Miss Bailey; we used to have to go across the playground and up the stairs to cookery. We had two Miss Bells, Ellen Bell and Joan Bell, they were two sisters. One was a music teacher. We had nothing to do with the boys, the boys were the other side. When we used to go to cookery and the people in the villages, the boys, used to come to the carpentry with Mr Savage over the other side. Of course that was great, we all liked to see the boys come in and we used to pop out the windows and drop a dish cloth so we could run down and pick it up. They were happy times, really.

There was a teacher who lived up Broad Street who used to ask me to take her books home. Instead of realising that I was stopping her from having to take them, I thought it was marvellous to go and take the books home and put them on her doorstep.

Beryl Wade

The head teacher was called Mr Underwood who we called Percy, very reverently I'm sure. My teacher most of the time was Mr Williams. He was very nice, he was one of the teachers who came down from London, you remember it was the wartime and they had evacuees, so I think he came down with a lot of the evacuees from London.

Val Gagen

We had several teachers, because you didn't move classes quite so much as they do today. Your teacher took you for most subjects. The one I can remember is a Mr Williams. He came down with the evacuees and he was a very good teacher, but you didn't mess him about. If he said something then you were expected to learn it. If you didn't, he wanted to know why not. It was very strict in those days.

Gwen Salmon

Teachers c1934 (including left to right)
PW Underwood (Head), BM Gurteen (School Manager) A Smith (Sportsmaster)

History Group

The first year I can remember my teacher being a lady called Mrs Jackson; a very tall lady. She was really nice, one of the ones that will stick in my head forever. In the first year I can remember a tray of chicks coming in at Easter, little baby fluffy chicks and I can remember having a fascination with Mrs Jackson's socks. She wore knee length socks underneath her trousers which were multicoloured stripes. When she used to sit reading stories, I used to roll the socks down. She used to let me roll them down her leg and pull them back up again. Whether that's a fetish I don't know. I've not had it since, but I do remember that.
The next year I had a lady and for the life of me cannot remember her name, which is awful. I actually bumped into her at my son's Christmas fête this year and she actually pulled me up and recognised me. She said, "Do you remember I was your second year teacher, Jane?" and I did.
My next teacher was a lady called Miss Elliott who I said had Timotei hair, very long, blonde, straight, flyaway hair and I always wanted to have hair like hers. As you can see, I've got dark, curly hair so I was a bit upset that it didn't turn out long and straight and blonde.
My last teacher was a lady, Mrs Farrow, and she stuck in my mind. She's been one of the teachers that I've always looked up to as well. Unfortunately, I found out a few years ago that she'd died, which was quite upsetting. She taught everything, but I can remember every day she would just pick one like the seven times table and she would only give you enough time to get your pencil out and then we would have to do it.
My first teacher had such an impression on me, she was just so lovely. I actually got a chance to meet her again later on when I was Samuel Ward Upper School, because I'd done a course which was called community service at the time, where we would go to a particular school and help out. I went to Place Farm and one particular day they were out on a field trip and they took me to Cangle School and said I had to go into whatever classroom it was. I couldn't believe she was still there and it was so nice and we gave each other a hug and said hello. I can't believe out of all the children that she remembered me. It was quite important that she'd remembered me.

Jane Duffy

Miss Castle was very much loved by all the pupils. It was a great compliment to me as a teacher one day when some child growled at me, "You're nearly as bad as Miss Castle". She's also no longer with us. I think she became deputy at Castle Manor and there is still a prize giving annually in her name.

Hazel Smith

I can remember some of the teachers' names. There was Miss Kellar, that was the nice one, that was the last class. Then there was Miss Gowers, she taught the English. Miss Gent was needlework. Then there was Mrs Leach and Miss Cutmoor, and they were the little children's ones. Mrs Royce and a Mrs Duckley. I can't remember who took us for cookery. We used to do cookery once a week, which was right round the other side of the building in a room upstairs, but I can't remember who the teacher was.

Rose Philips

What I remember of Miss Martin was, she was OK, a nice teacher. She actually taught my daughter when she went there. She was married then, she was Mrs Edwards. My daughter's 28 now.

When I was about 6, I remember moving to another class and Mrs Gillespie was my teacher. I really feared this woman. I remember taking up a piece of paper with drawings on and she got hold of me and shook me and I still don't know to this day why, what I'd done. I can always remember being hit. That wasn't the first time. It was usually over petty things. I found her an awful woman, I've never forgotten her name. When I was her class I didn't enjoy that at all; it was definitely learning in fear. The next class was Miss Newitt's, again a smashing lady. Once when I went to the dentist's, I had about three fillings. When I came back, she gave me three pence for each one.

I was there right up until I was 11. When I was there, it was the infants, juniors and seniors. So you actually left there when you were 15. I can remember the seniors, because when I was 8 I was in Mrs Shelley's class. She was a good teacher as well. When I was in the juniors, you went round the back where you played. There were seniors there as well, so I can remember them. Then they built the new Castle Manor. My brother thinks he was amongst the first to go to the new school. I went to the new one when I was 11.

You had a form teacher all the time. You didn't have different teachers. The headmistress was Mrs Potter. I had a Miss Honeycombe, she was very strict. And we had a Mrs Greensleeves, she was another awful teacher.

Peter Isaacs

My first head was Mr Clayton. I think my first teacher was Miss Wallace. From Miss Wallace we went to Mrs Hiner and then Mr Ready. Archie Smith took classes one and two and that was where we finished up. Classes one and two were in the same room and we had the House of Lords with five of the head boys, you might say. There was also a Mr Hines. If anybody played truant he used to come round to the house.

Ted Basham

We had some lovely teachers. One was Mr Eddy. Miss Emerson, she came from Clare. Then we had a hired lady, Mrs Hiner. The last teacher I had was Mr Smith, Archie Smith, who was an Echo reporter.
Mrs Hiner, in the classroom where she was, had a wastepaper basket and she had a slate on there and she had a little methylated spirit stove. We used to have to take it in turns to fill this tin kettle up. Then she used to light that and then she and this other lady, Miss Emerson, used to have a cup of Ovaltine in the morning. In the afternoon, they had a cup of tea. Whoever was on that day to do this job, sometimes we ran out of methylated spirits and we used to have to go up to Paul's, the ironmonger's, and have it filled up with methylated spirits. Then we had to wash up their two cups. The tin kettle didn't last long and sometimes, whoever was on the job that day, perhaps the kettle had run and we used to have to go up to Paul's and get a new one. That was 51/2d. I don't know if they make them now. The stove smelt, you could smell the methylated spirits. None of the male teachers had any drinks or anything like that.

Percy Sizer

We had Archie Smith, he was reporter for the Echo at that time of day. He was a real schoolteacher. He was strict. If there was anything you hadn't done in your programme which you had to do during the day, you had to stop in after school and do it. They used to stop there and see you doing it. If you had to write anything out, you had to write 500 lines or 100 lines and the teacher still stopped there until you'd done it.

Harold Sozer

The teachers were Underwood, Smith, Gant, Hooper and Hiner. Archie Smith was the sort of "play up and play the game" type of bloke. Gant was the captain in the First World War, he was Captain Gant. He lived up Wratting Road. I don't know much about Hooper. Mannie Hiner was a strict woman because I sat here and a bloke sat there and I wasn't thinking about anything and she went to smack him on the ear and he ducked and she hit me in the ear and knocked me off my chair. I can remember that as if it were yesterday.

Cyril Nunn

I remember being with Mrs Beer. Mrs Beer was a lovely lady, and her husband ran the grocery shop in the middle of the High Street, and it was a bit more upmarket than the Co-op. They had no children, and my sister said that Mrs Beer lives in Frinton, is ninety and is still alive.
Mr. Shelley was the top teacher in the infants. I can remember that he was tall and that he had tight curly hair. We sat on wooden desks that were in pairs, and the seat lifted up and they had an inkwell. I can remember it being very messy and getting ink everywhere.
There was a Miss Castle who did games. She probably did other things as well, and she was a Welsh lady. Smallish build, very likable and there again I liked games. Of course if you like something the teacher perhaps quite often they are more bias towards the children who were good at their subject. Then there was a Mr Williams and they are all I can remember from the senior school. There was a Miss Phillips who took us for cookery, and she also took needlework, because you did both together. I did all these things at home with my mother and grandmother, as well as knitting. One of the girls said that she learned to knit with Mrs Beer, but I remember learning to knit when I was about six with my grandmother.

Diane Basham

Mr Bartholomew said in class that Miss Potter won't be here this term, she's broken her leg and we all cheered. He said that we shouldn't cheer. We used to like Mr Bartholomew.

Bob Pavely

Miss Gowers was the one for Shakespeare. We used to have to sing "Come onto the yellow sands and there take hands" and "Where the bee sucks there suck I". She did poetry as well. "I must go down to the sea again, to the lonely sea and the sky".

Muriel Moore

I can remember my first teacher was a lady called Mrs Shelley and her husband was a teacher there as well. He died a couple years back, so he lived quite a long time. Mrs Shelley was one of the infant teachers.
I think teachers were stricter then. You were afraid of the teachers. One teacher was very strict, Mr Knock, he was very strict. He was quite a big man, quite thick set, and he used to shout at the boys a lot. I think even the boys were afraid of him. Then there were the teachers that you get round, like Miss Castle. She used to pretend she was strict, but she wasn't really. She used to like the girls. She used to be more of a friend to all the girls. She was a lovely lady. She was very tiny and perhaps that's why we

didn't take her seriously. I think we were all bigger than her anyway.
Miss Phillips, the cookery teacher, could be quite strict. If you peeled your potatoes too thick then you had to peel the peelings. I've had to do that before, because she'd come round and inspect the peelings when you peeled them. You couldn't waste any potato at all.

Hilary Filben

When I lived in London, all the teachers were female, so I remember having a male teacher for the very first time, Mr Logan. He was very soft. That's one thing I've found out about male teachers. He was putty. The next teacher we had was a male teacher, Mr Criddenden, and he was the same.
You'd have a form teacher who taught you every subject. It's not until you get to the older school that you go to different classes. We had a main classroom, and we'd come out and go to the hall for lunch and then PE elsewhere. We had assembly in the hall as well.

Julie Smith

My first teacher was Miss Wallace and then a Miss Duxbury. I must have been 6 years old when I was in Miss Duxbury's class. I remember quite a few of the teachers.
We had the evacuees when the war came and they brought several teachers with them. I recollect Mrs Martini and Mr Schonberg. Mr Williams, I think, came with the evacuees and Mr Bartholomew. I can't think who was head teacher when I started school, but I know it was Miss Potter in later years
I sat my 11+ exam when I was Mrs Martini's class and I failed. Mrs Martini couldn't understand why. She lived two doors away from where I lived in Chayney Pieces at that time. They assumed it was because I said I didn't want to go because none of my friends was going. So I stayed on at the Cangle school until I left. When I left I was in Mr Williams' class.

Muriel Moore

The first teacher I had was Miss Wallace who later became Mrs Farr and then there was Miss Large. In the juniors there was Mrs Beer, Mr Dunt and Mr Hooper. I was never in Archie Smith's class, but he was the Echo reporter at the time after he left school. He was a good shot with a piece of chalk, because if any of the lads in the school had their mouth open he would pitch a piece of chalk right in the mouth. Then there was Mrs Hiner the school Nanny, who used to take us for singing lessons. I was in the choir for the different plays we put on, Merchant of Venice, Midsummer Night's Dream.
Then when I went up to the seniors, I went to 1A which was Miss Castle. Mr Underwood was the headmaster. After that I went into Mr Williams' class which was

the top class, 3A. I was never in the B classes, always in the A classes. He used to be a man who talked through his teeth, and he used to say, "We are now going down the garden. Anyone not wishing to go please say so, and I will give them some arithmetic". Everybody used to go down the garden.

Robert Pavely

There was a big chap about 6ft 6, ex-boxer called Williams. He used to take physics and history. Everybody was scared stiff of him. He was one of the old school. He just walked around the classroom quietly and cuffed anybody's ear who wasn't paying attention as he walked past. At least after he'd done it once everybody behaved themselves. Then there was a Canadian ex-military chap called John Knock who used to take geography. There was also a Miss Phillips, another spinster. Those two lived together. She used to teach cookery and needlework.

There was another teacher called Hiner. He died almost as soon as I arrived at Haverhill school. I can't even remember what his subject was. Then the woodwork master was a chap called J.O. Savoury, known affectionately as Joss to everyone. He had taught three generations of our family so he was getting a bit old in the tooth.

The metalwork master at that time was an ex-airforce chap who's name was Whittaker. I got on extremely well with him. He had a very old Jaguar car. When there were subjects like physics which I didn't much care for, he would have an urgent job to do and I used to go out and make spare parts on the lathe for his car.

There was another ex-airforce chap by the name of Reynolds who took science. He was an extremely good shot with a piece of chalk if you were talking or not paying attention. There were a few like that. John Knock was particularly good with one of those big, heavy, wooden-backed rubbers and he used to hurl those at people.

Then we had a real comedian called Hunter who was the gardening master. He had a very dry sense of humour. He used to get me onto the school gardens driving a tractor and things like that. But in lessons he was particularly funny. If he thought half the class was dozing off because they were getting bored, he'd come up with one of his funny little stories. For example, in a very dry drought season, we always plant our onions between our rows of potatoes. The reason for that is that the onions will make the potatoes eyes water and give them moisture. That was the sort of thing he would throw in at odd moments.

Another chap, ex-airforce, was Farrow. He taught a bit of everything; a bit of sport and that. Another one who was there a long time, he started there almost the same time as me; a chap called McGregor who was the art teacher. He went on to be very, very old. He's still around in fact. We also had a young ex-airforce PTI instructor called Duckett. You always got your one or two soft touches, like a chap called Wiseman who could never keep control of the class. He taught English part-time. Because he could never keep control of the class, he had a very hard time. People used to draw things on his blackboard when his back was turned, and also tie his bike up to the roof in the bicycle shed or let his tyres down. That was all part of school fun.

Captain Dunt who was ex-military was a great big man, about 17 or 18 stone. There was Mrs Beer and then a Mr and Mrs Shelley, they were in the junior school. Then Betty and Reg Carr, they were also in the junior school.

Tony Stevens

There is one teacher I can recall and I think his name was Mr Roy, but it might have been Roy something. He was the teacher of 4A and he seemed to be more of a lively, interesting teacher. It was quite enjoyable being in his class.

Gerry Kiernan

When I was at the school the headmaster was Mr Underwood, and the deputy head teacher was Miss Castle and then there was a music teacher called Mr Kibble and a man who taught gardening called Mr Hunter and then there was Mr Harvey who taught science and there was a teacher called Miss Eape, who still lives in Haverhill and is called Mrs Smith and then there was a Miss Phillips who taught cookery and only the girls went to cookery, the boys weren't allowed to do cookery, only the girls did cookery. And then there was Mr Williams and there was a Mr Savory who taught woodwork and the boys all went to woodwork, so you didn't do the same things, the boys did woodwork and the girls did cookery and then there was Mr Farrow, and Mr Jones who taught PE and games and also Mr Wiseman, and Mr Shelley, he lived in Haverhill and he's now in an old person's home. Mr Knock taught maths and Mr McGregor taught art and still lives in Haverhill and then there's Mr Whittaker who taught metalwork, there you are, all of them.

Michael leedale

My very first teacher was called Miss Bridger and, if someone had been naughty, she used to make them stand in the corner. I don't think she ever did that to me, but she did to some of the other children. There was a teacher called Mr Garnett, there was a teacher called Mrs Newitt, there was a teacher called Mr Wheatley. There was one teacher, I think it was Miss Bridger, who if we weren't paying attention in class, she used to say 'stop hibernating children'. If we were gazing out the window and not getting on with our lessons, she used to tell us to stop hibernating, I remember her saying that.

I was here for six years, so I would have been with six different teachers. I would think there was probably about 10 or 12 classes with 35 in a class.

Some were quite funny and some were quite friendly, some were quite helpful, in fact they were all quite helpful really, so yeah, I liked them all I think really.

I think my favourite teacher was called Mr Wheatley. He taught us when we were about 10 or 11, so I think he was probably my favourite one.

Geoffrey Ship

Miss Marian Castle was 2A Form Mistress, all 5' 2" of her with short hair. With a yellow jumper and green gym slip she could have been so easily mistaken for a pupil! She never suffered fools gladly irrespective of the pupil size, she laid down the law in no uncertain way.

Mrs Martinez was 2B Form Mistress who arrived from London with the evacuees a well dressed, well spoken lady. I recall her reciting the poem 'The Golden Journey to Samark and'. The movement of her hands, variations in her voice - she lived the part. I have often wondered what she would have said had she ever known the lasting impact it had on one of her youngsters.

Reg Herrington

THE HEAD TEACHER

He always seemed to be a very imposing sort of figure. A very jolly sort of person with glasses, and he lived in the house which was at the side of the Cangle then. When we did The Tempest and Midsummer Night's Dream, the photographs were taken in his garden, his little lawn at the side of his house. He was a very nice person really.

Gladys Ely

Pupils & Headteacher *History Group*

In my day Mr Williams was the head teacher, Percy Williams. He was a fine man, I liked him very much. He'd encouraged most of the boys, very encouraging all the way round. Mr Williams also was a good master, very fair; strict, firm but fair.

Derek Bacon

The headmaster was Mr Underwood. He was a nice man, very fair. At the end of every term we had a big assembly and he always had his favourite hymn, "The day Thou gavest, Lord, is ended" and I always remember him through that. There was a Miss Castle and those two used to be on the rostrum to see us all off and wish us a happy holiday.

Gwen Salmon

There was a flight of stairs near the toilets and there was this really lovely tiled floor section and I think it was near to where the headmaster used to live. I think he lived on the end and these stairs went up and you never dared to go there. I think that's where all the admin staff were in their offices. But you never went up there unless a teacher actually asked you to physically take something, which wasn't very often. You used to go in twos, you'd never go on your own because it was upstairs and the headmaster's up there and everything. I think I can remember seeing him twice the whole time I was there. I always thought he must be a really scary man until I actually saw him and he was quite small, with grey hair.

Jane Duffy

When I was a pupil there were two completely separate schools, the secondary modern school and the infant and junior school. Miss Potter was head of the infant and junior with her sister who was her secretary. They were really well known characters in the town. Mr Underwood was head of the upper school, secondary modern as it was known then, and they worked completely independently.

The first day I came for the interview I sat in Mr Underwoods study and there was a photograph above his desk of him with a football team, and the date on it was the year I was born, and there he sat and he didn't look any different. He lived in the schoolhouse that looks onto Wratting road. That room on the end nearest to the main driveway in there now, that was his sitting room. I don't know when he moved out. He went on to be the first head at Castle Manor.

It could have been quite difficult when we had the two head teachers, because their two studies were in what had been the old caretaker's house. You would go in through an outside door from the front and Mr Underwood's study was on one side of the door and Miss Potter's was on the other. The stairs went straight up in front, little twisty stairs which would go up to the staff room, so that if you were wanting to go to the staff room at break time, and there were people waiting to see either of the heads, it was quite a chaotic corner there for a bit.

The thing that was really interesting, I thought, was that the head of the secondary modern school lived in the schoolhouse, which was at the infant school end of the building. I often wondered why it was that he had the schoolhouse and why didn't the head of the infant/junior have the house. When I came, he had been here for a long time. He said to me that when he first came they had told him he was a lucky man, he was going to have a new school. I think it had been about twenty years and he still hadn't got it. The new school, when it came, was Castle Manor and he was only head for a little while, then he was ill and retired.

Hazel Smith

The headmaster was Mr Wilson to begin with. After two years he retired and we had Mr Underwood. The caretaker was Mr Scrivener and he was also the ambulance man. So if anyone was ill or had done anything he used to look after them. The headmistress of the infants and the girls school was Miss Cahrer.

Percy Sizer

When I started there first the headmaster was Mr Clayton, a little short fellow with a tiny moustache, a Charlie Chaplin moustache. I hadn't been there long and then we had Mr Wilson, tubby Wilson we used to call him. He came there for a while. When I got towards the top class we had Mr Underwood.

Harold Sozer

My headmistress was a Miss Potter and she was a large lady who lived in the road called Broad Street near to the school. Mr Underwood was the head of the seniors and he was a very lovely man, and did very much for his school and his children.
It was the head of the senior school who lived in the schoolhouse which was in the same grounds as the Cangle, and that was on the end of the Infants/Juniors.

Diane Basham

Head & Pupils 1920 *History Group*

I can remember Mr Danes and Mr Hutchinson and they're the only two names I can remember. Mr Hutchinson was the headmaster at the time and Mr Danes was the deputy head because he went on to be headmaster of Chalkstone, I think it was. Mr Hutchinson was very much a shambling figure. He always had a suit on but he was like Patrick Moore, always in a suit but ill-fitting. I can remember his retirement, we gave him a set of golf clubs. Mr Danes was younger and dark-haired and a very much deeper voice, very loud. I liked him and I think he was quite respected.

Karen Clark

The head lady teacher at that time was a little short woman about 5ft nothing called Marian Castle who used to take English and also swimming. She was a right little fire piece, not much of her but she would still clout anyone's ear who got the wrong side of her.
The headmistress was a very large lady with a very short haircut and big glasses, called Pansy Potter. She used to wear these crocheted stockings.

Tony Stevens

Mr Hutchinson was the head teacher. He came over as a very strict, daunting figure. You never saw the head teacher that much at that time.

Gerry Kiernan

We were in awe of Mr Hutchinson, the head. Having known him later, he's quite a sweetie, but at the time he seemed terrifying, because he seemed to have such a stern

face. And the glasses were either gold-rimmed or metal-rimmed and they always seemed rather stern.
I had to go and see him once because we were making a peg bag and I was supposed to have brought in a coat hanger and I'd forgotten mine, being organised. The teacher said, go and ask Mr Hutchinson if you can go home and get it, because I only lived at Down's Crescent. It wasn't far, it would be about a four or five minute walk. But the thought of having to go and ask him was terrifying. But he said yes and I could go.

Jane Farrow

As a child, I can remember the headmistress, she was very plump, she was not married, she was very stern and we were a little bit afraid of her and her name was Miss Potter, and she sat in her office all day long and if you ever did anything wrong, you were sent to Miss Potter and she was very, very cross with you. She had a way of looking at you and you would shake in your shoes. She had a sister there, Miss Ethel Potter, who was her secretary, so it was quite a family and Miss Ethel Potter had charge of all the books .... and if you wanted one, you had to go and ask Miss Ethel Potter which was almost as bad as going to see the headmistress.

Marion Gregory

When I first started it was a lady called Miss Potter. I think she'd been here a long time, because she used to say to everybody, I remember teaching your father or I remember teaching your mother and then when I was about eight or nine, we had a man called Mr Hutchinson who came and he then went on to be head of Chalkstone Middle School and Mr Hutchinson introduced lots of new ideas. He got the boys football team started up, which we never had before and he used to take us out on school trips.

Geoffrey Ship

Mr Underwood lived in the School House at the Wratting Road end, and he told me himself that he had never locked his doors the whole of his time there! Those really were the days!

Alan Haigh

Mr Underwood the Head was a bespectacled, balding man with an ever ready smile, always the gentleman hence he was liked and respected by staff and pupils.
Mr Williams was the Deputy Head, a tall auburn haired man of few words always to the point and one look was adequate to maintain discipline.

Reg Herrington

DISCIPLINE

Discipline was quite fierce. Most of the men had a slipper that they would administer. I know as a very junior teacher, if some of the lads really annoyed me I could quite freely send him to one of the men to ask to borrow the slipper, and he would come back rubbing his backside. It didn't happen very often, but it was an option that could happen. There were obviously the ones who were always a pain, but it wasn't that bad. It was generally a very friendly sort of place.

Hazel Smith

Our school teachers were very strict. If you got in trouble down at the school, you daren't come home and tell your parents because you'd get another clip round the ear. But now today, if anybody does anything, the parents go down and get onto the schoolteachers. That doesn't make sense to me. Mr Ready would get his thumb and he'd dig it in your ribs. Miss Webb, she was another one, she used to get the ruler and strike you with it.

Ted Basham

The School was strict. When Mrs Hiner came round to you, she had a habit of digging one of her fingers in your back. Then the lady from Clare, Miss Emerson, she used to have you out the front and rap your knuckles with a ruler.

Percy Sizer

We used to get the cane now and again. The headmaster had a great big box there with all the thick ones and thin ones. He'd give you a wallop. And it was no good going home and tell your parents because they'd say it served you right, you must have done something wrong and you'd get another hit round the ear.

Harold Sozer

I was often punished so that was nothing new really. You'd get the cane, that's what would happen probably. It didn't do me any harm.
If you were in assembly and someone moved, Mr Smith would be after them straightaway. I've known a lad get a terrible clout just for that. Someone might have given him a push or something like that, he was quite nasty. You were on your toes as far as discipline went. There was no answering back that I remember. The singing class was the only one that got slightly out of hand. All the rest of the classes were very well controlled. In fact, there were no problems at all with them. I can't remember ever that a class got out of control or answering back, that sort of thing.

Derek Bacon

Talking secretly was always being done and when my mate and I were so engrossed in our secret conversation that we failed to spot the Geography teacher creeping up behind us, he grabbed our two heads in his hands and tried to push them together. We managed to grit our teeth to resist his strong grip and stop our heads from being knocked together so that it didn't hurt, well not too much anyway.

Roy Brazier

I don't recall any punishments. I must have been a good boy, I think! I think the cane was still in use, but it was probably in the headmaster's study as a deterrent, but it was very rarely used I think.

Val Gagen

I can remember standing on a chair, for laughing; things used to make me laugh and I have got perhaps a carrying voice and I was always picked up. I had to stand on a chair for this particular teacher. She was a very hard teacher. She didn't last long so I think she was complained about, because she was very strict. Standing on a chair for an hour. My legs killed me afterwards. I never told my mother because I'd probably have got a clout for being naughty in the first place. But you mostly had lines. We weren't very often hit with the ruler. We had one teacher, if she saw you messing about, she'd rattle you, as she went by, with the ruler on the knuckles or clip you round the ear, not hard but just to let you know that she was there and she was watching. It didn't do any harm, I don't think there's enough it, I really don't. Because I think that's why teachers are not quite so respected today as they were then. You never thought about messing your teacher. She was up there to teach you and you didn't cheek back. If you did, you were in trouble from her and you'd get another one when you got home because a letter would go with you to say what had happened. So you were very careful what you did. They say corporal punishment, but there was never much metered out. No one was ever really caned. It was mostly you went before the headmaster and that was punishment enough, to be told and go and see the headmaster was the pits really. You really had done bad.

Gwen Salmon

I can remember being told that caning was a punishment at Cangle, but never knew anybody that had it. I didn't have it myself. So whether it was still in place when I went there, I don't really know. But I do remember the rumours going about that caning was in.

Jane Duffy

I think we used to stand outside the door. I can remember the last room because the room was next to the governess' room.

Rose Philips

My parents used to give me plenty of wallops. I've got three children and I never hit one of them and they're all academics now.
I never hit any of my kids because I didn't want them to have what I had. I used to shout a lot. And they're fine, they're just great. They all play as well. When they do come home and we're all together, we have a good old ceilidh session. And they've all been to the Cangle as well. The kids are just fine, we communicate lovely. Whereas with my parents, you couldn't have a conversation in case you said the wrong thing. Children have got to have freedom, got to have fun.
There was one chap who was in the infants with me, he was a case. He never changed all through, he was wild. When he left school he was always in trouble with the law. It didn't do him any good at all, all this caning. He used to get it quite regular, he was always in trouble. But he was a nice chap to talk to. Maybe they made him what he is.

Peter Isaacs

It was all hard work more or less. They were strict. I don't think they're so strict today. If you got a clip of the ear, well that was it, you got a clip of the ear, you'd done wrong. Now, they don't correct them. They're not allowed to. I don't think it did children any harm if it was done within reason. It never hurt us.

Cyril Nunn

There was a lot of respect for the teachers. I can't remember it being strict so that you were frightened of it. Then again, I liked school. In those days you did as you were told. You had the odd rebel but there wasn't that much trouble at the school. I think that because we went through the infants and junior when it was wartime, there was a community spirit amongst everybody.

Diane Basham

I was punished for quite a lot of things, mainly talking. All of my school reports say, "she could do better" or "she talks too much". It's only when you leave school that you realise that you did talk too much. I suppose I could have done better. I did alright, I got by, I was never bottom of the class or anything, but then I was never top of the class either.
I remember many a time standing in the school corridor being sent out of class. All the children's coats used to hang in the corridor, so if I heard the headmaster coming along I used to hide in the coats so he wouldn't see me. Not just me, there were several of us.

We didn't get the cane, but the teachers were strict. I remember in religious instruction class, one of the boys wasn't listening and the teacher had the Bible in her hands. She crept up behind him and she banged him on the head with it. She said, "if you won't listen to the word of the Lord, then feel it".

Hilary Filben

I don't think punishment did any harm. In fact, they gain complete respect from the class because you knew if you played them up, what you would get. So they didn't have any disruption in the classroom, they just didn't. This Wiseman chap was the only one who was a soft touch and he had a terrible time. This is really what the problem is with classrooms today. If children can get away with it, they'll get away with it. We were always brought in a strict sort of regime. If we got into trouble at school, or out of school, if the teacher didn't discipline us our parents would. So we were going to get it one way or the other. I don't think it did anybody any harm. There's one thing to give you a sharp smack in the right place at the right time, especially in front of a class of your friends, that's the quickest way of cutting you down to size. The cane was only used on very rare occasions and then, of course, the culprit was sent round to the headmaster's office. You had to do something quite extreme to warrant the cane.

Tony Stevens

Lots of people had the slipper and the cane. The teachers used to hit people with the slipper and the head used to give people the cane, but you had to be really bad to get the cane. I got the slipper because I was talking in the dining room. They were very, very strict. There were very strict rules. At lunch time there used to be two minutes silence and you weren't allowed to talk at all, and you had to all line up in the playground in silence when it was time to come in and all sorts of silly rules about your exercises - you had to underline things and make sure you put everything in the margin. It was very strict and you had to call the teacher Sir, when you answered the register, you had to say yes sir, or miss. It wasn't friendly like it is now.

Michael Teedale

I remember my dad telling me when he came to school that in the morning all the children had to line up and they had to hold out their hands and the teacher used to walk down the line to check that their fingernails were clean and that their shoes were clean and if their fingernails were dirty or their shoes were dirty, they used to get over the hands with a stick. But they didn't do that when I was there, so I think it was probably stricter long ago than what it was when I went there.

Geoffrey Ship

If you wanted to go to the toilet, you had to ask permission, put your hand up to ask to leave the room. And before you went back into that room again, you had to knock the door and ask permission to go in. That was real strict then, wasn't it?

Harold Sozer

When writing out lines as a punishment, three or four pens were joined tightly with rubber-bands to enable us to write several lines at once, but we had been rumbled in this respect and instead of 100 lines of "I must not offer rude remarks" we had to write out about twenty pages from a book, so our very own patent line-writer was of no use.

Roy Brazier

Headmasters House & urinal, Station Road *Jean & Bob Pavely*

PUPILS AND FRIENDS

I still see old pupils now, some of them are still around and there are quite a few of us unfortunately that have passed on. In fact, two still live over here and they used to be the "Kiddie" twins and Anne lives over here and Helen just lives a few doors up along there. Jack Riggs was our comedian, he was very good in plays, he was excellent as an actor. He only lives just up North Avenue.
A lot of out of town children used to come to the school in those days from one or two little villages.

Gladys Ely

The five of us from Kedington were soon named 'Out Towners'. There was John Gowers a local publicans son, Valentine Gagen gamekeepers son, Tony Mayes, Derek Bacon the village Policeman's son and myself. Most pupils answered to a nickname, how they originated still remains a mystery. 'Baner', 'Tilly', 'Sos', 'Bomber', 'Mivet', 'Gabby' and 'Gorgon'. Who would be brave to use them now?

Reg Herrington

A friend I had was Beryl Davy. She was one of several sisters, she was the youngest one, she was the same age as me. Her father had a photography studio and that was in the high street. It was almost exactly next door to the town hall. It was a really long, low, rambling old house. It must have dated back to the 1600's I should think. It was a lovely place, it was all beams. He had his studio at the front and they lived at the back. You went up the side of the house into a yard, like a courtyard, and their house was shaped like a 'T'. We used to dance to records, that was when I was about 15. Beryl married a doctor and now lives in Chicago.

Christine Hart

There was Eileen next door. You see Haverhill in those days was very confined, it wasn't so outlandish as it is now, so most people lived not very far from the school. Up here there was Eileen Beavis, Freddie Mays, Peggy Pool, Charlie Metcalf, Sylvia Preston, Cleave Preston, her twin sisters, the Tuck family, Winnie, Hilda, Violet, Tommy Mays. All these houses were full of children and they were very near the school. My friend lived up Hazel Stubbs, which is going up the hill towards Sainsbury's, Doris Turner she was then. I'm still in contact with some of them. Some unfortunately are not here any longer. Eileen still lives next door.

Beryl Wade

I remember Grace was my best friend. She lived opposite for a time and we used to get on very well. We are on a par, she was better at Maths than I was and I was better at English than she was but that's how we used to work. There was a girl there called Thelma. I see some in the street and we have a laugh still. A lot of them are local still and that's nice. A lot of the teachers are not. Obviously, they're a lot older, a lot have gone now, moved away. Because some came down here with the evacuees and when they went back they went with them. But some settled, some did like it here. They got used to the quiet and quite enjoyed it.

Gwen Salmon

I had friends called Denise Farrant, Laura Marks, Jane Fowler who was part of the Fowlers who were in Haverhill there at the newsagent's, Darren Beers and a chap called Michael, can't ever remember his surname. A lot of them are either still about or they've come back and I've bumped into them, so that's really nice. Oh, Matthew Austin, because he was the one that bought me the purse with the beads on, I can't forget him, even though I did bite the beads off.

Jane Duffy

With the over-spill from London we were having rather different children coming in. They moved quicker, they thought quicker, it was very interesting for a while.
They tended to come in gradually, and at first they would appear to be one of the over-spill. One or two were a bit different, but they mixed in very well eventually. At first we did notice that they did tend to run circles around some of the locals. Of course we had the buses all in from the villages, we had the Thurlows and Keddingtons, and we even had some Bumpstead at that time.
The buses all used to park for loading out in Withersfield Road. The children would line up just inside the railings and then we would see them onto the buses there.

I suppose there must have been around 400 pupils, but I wouldn't like to say for certain. It was quite a lot, and of course the infants and juniors were a separate school although within the same building. So we had staggered break and lunch times.
Some of my pupils were Geoff Farrant who's now got the electrician's business; there was Paul Bailey the builder; the Deeks family. One of the Deeks family was in my class, they came from Kedington.

Hazel Smith

My friend at school was Robert Paxman. Unfortunately he died when he was only 16, we went up through different classes together. I knew Robert Hunt, Barry Basham, Sid Stocking, John Wright and the girls Jennifer Jobson, Annette Moore, Sheila, Brenda, Diana Flint.

Summer holiday friends were Robert Paxman, Robert Hunt, John Baker. I don't know why, but the river seemed to be always full and we used to build a raft on the river. We used to catch sticklebacks and go vaulting over the river with a stick. My grandad used to work at the gasworks. My parents were strict, so if I got soaking wet I would stop at the gasworks and strip off and grandad would dry all my clothes out next to the ovens.

Peter Isaacs

I remember Jack Fake, Bill Jobson, Alan Claydon, Morris Page, Bert Sutherland, Ben Spicer, Jack Whiting, Jimmy Mansfield, we were all friends together. And the girls were Becky Binks, Gertie Farrant, Grace Judd, Rhona Judd, Olive Jennings. A lot of them are dead now. There aren't many Haverhill people left. I'm one of the lucky ones really.

Percy Sizer

Pupils *Mrs Iron*

In 1945, they started bussing children in from the village schools, when we were both at Sudbury, and because there were too many children in the junior school, the brightest ones of us were moved up two terms. I seem to remember these village children because they were all strangers to us. We knew the children who were in the class we went into because they had been the class above us, and then they brought these children in from the villages. About three years ago I was speaking to a girl, and I felt that she was one of the village girls. She said that they were disadvantaged being from these village schools where they had only two teachers for the whole school, and that made them so behind academically. Some of them never really caught up.

Diane Basham

There was a boy called Ronald Hobby who I've lost sight of. There was Diane Basham. There was Greta Tuck and Eleanor Daniels who I met a little while ago. Janet Onion, who's now a teacher herself. Greta Bradnor, a cousin who was a year younger than me. Tony Carr and Brian Hall were the ones who lived near us.

Jean Pavely

My husband joined the school round about the same time as I did, maybe a little bit later. He had a female teacher, Miss, or Mrs, Scott, who he tells me he didn't like very much. She left shortly after to have a baby and never came back.
I think the very first friend I had was called Carol Elliott because she lived nearby and we became friends. Julie Thomas, Linda Watkins, I can remember quite a few. I don't really see any of them now. We still send cards to one or two. We have a reunion from the Upper School every ten years.

Julie Smith

Lorna Withers was my best friend at Cangle. She used to live up Broad Street which was that street next to the school. On the corner of that street there was a house and they had a Mina bird in a cage in the garden. All the kids used to go past before and after school and talk to this minor bird. I think it was taught some swearwords as well. I remember any time she was late for school, she'd come down the back of her house and skip over the wall and get in that way. We got to be friendly because my surname at the time was Williats, so on the register we were right at the bottom. I was friends with her for quite a long while. I don't know what she's doing now. She was my bestest friend there, you know.
We were together nearly all the time actually, so it was probably to the exclusion of most other people, to be honest. Her nan had a house out on the road that comes out of Haverhill towards Cambridge, which has all been redeveloped now anyway. It was right by a river and we always used to go and play there. I always fell in the river. Lorna had older brothers, so they were there as well. I never really had a lot to do with my sister at school, because by the time she started in infants, I was in juniors and you didn't mix. And that happened throughout school-life.

Karen Clark

I remember a family called the Patrick family that lived at Haverhill Hall, there were about five or six children of varying ages and they all came to Haverhill school. Their father was a very outstanding character, a huntsman and everything. If any of his children got reprimanded, he would come down to the school on his horse and duck his head and ride straight in the classroom and actually threaten the schoolmaster with his hunting crop.
One of my closest friends was a chap called Roger Kenny. His father was in the airforce at RAF Straddishall. They were Irish by original, but they lived at Straddishall and we always got on extremely well in all the time that he was there. His elder brother, Derry Kenny, was the same age as my brother and they've still been friends for the last 40 years. He's coming over from New Zealand next week to stay for 6 weeks. He had film star looks, Derry Kenny and all the girls tried to get a date with him.
Another lifelong friend was a chap called Geoffrey Hughes who came from Helion's

Bumpstead. We started school on the same day and we left on the same day. He still lives in Haverhill. He works for the council. He came from an ordinary working family and he worked on farms and eventually finished up working for the council doing grass cutting. He must be nearly due for retirement now.
Another farmer, Michael Jacobs, he came from Helion's Bumstead. His father later bought a farm in Clare. There was another one called Roy Gregory, he started school the same time as me, he went on to be a farm manager. His father worked for an uncle of mine. On my mother's side, they owned nearly all the farms in Helion's Bumstead. All farms had a lot of employees in those days.

Tony Stevens

My friends were Kerry Jane, who went through school with me. There was a very tall girl called Janet Lloyd; Neil Matthews, Anthony Rolds, Trevor Hyatt whose children I see and teach, Caroline Bennett, Karen Robinson who I went to speech therapy with. There was a Greek boy called Arthur and I can't remember his surname.

Jane Farrow

I had two special friends, Margaret and Muriel their names were, and I'm still friendly with them both, 50 plus years on and I can remember playing in the playground with them and three children together is not always a very good idea, because they quite often fell out with me and they'd go off on their own and leave me by myself, and I can remember feeling a bit lonely sometimes, but sometimes Margaret and I used to be friends and Muriel wasn't being loved and she would go off on her own, and it's not till you get older that you think to yourself, it wasn't very nice really to do that to each other.

Marion Gregory

Adrian, he was my best friend all through the grammar school as well and there was someone called Colin .... I was very friendly with and Alan Radford, Michael Last. There was a lot of us who all stayed friends together and there were lots of new children came as well because when I was about eight, that was when people started to move into Haverhill from London so there were lots of new families came down, which was really good, because it meant there were lots of new friends for us all.

Geoffrey Ship

They were happy days really. Everyone knew everybody else in Haverhill then, because Haverhill was so small that you practically knew everyone. Everyone in your class was a neighbour or a friend, it was really nice.

Hilary Filben

GIRLS - BOYS

Boys? Oh I like them! I wasn't interested in them until I got into probably the third year, but it was more the last year, where we used to play something called the fly monkeys which somebody brought to my attention a few weeks ago. Basically it was just kiss chase, but we just decided to change the name of it to something different. I can remember having this thing for a boy at school. He went to Tenerife with his mum and he bought back a little purse with all these little glass beads on. I remember when we decided we weren't going to be together anymore, I bit all these glass beads off the purse.

There weren't any bike sheds to go behind, everything was done in the open. We used to do a lot of dancing, to Boney M in the lunch hour. We used to sing Brown Girl in the Ring and get in this ring.

Jane Duffy

I'm not sure if I should tell you this one really! Actually, she's lives up the road, her name is Annette. I wanted to see something and she showed me her belly button behind the bicycle sheds. But she wanted my Wagon Wheel first!

Peter Isaacs

We used to play with girls when we came out of school. We used to play hide and seek, and play mothers and fathers. We picked our own girl. We used to make a little house in gaps in the hedge. We used to pick up bits of saucers and plates and things. Somebody would say they were going to get married. So we'd make a dirt cake and then we'd pinch some of our mother's flour and put sugared candy all over them. The girl would have a piece of curtain over her head.

Percy Sizer

We did mix with boys, but a lot of the time, when we were younger they were a nuisance. They were always coming in and spoiling your games. They pushed in when you were trying to do something. Girls preferred to play on their own. If you'd got your beads in a nice tin and you were sorting them out, they'd come and kick them all over the place and that sort of thing. I don't think the girls mixed with the boys until we got older. We were there quite a lot of years in that school, from about 5 to 15. It was only in the latter years, I think, that you used to play games with the boys. They played cricket and football and that sort of thing.The boys had metalwork and woodwork. Girls did science, I can remember later on doing a bit of science. Girls were allowed to do that. Mostly the boys had their subjects and the girls had theirs.

Hilary Filben

There was some mixing, but I was always in groups of girls. I never mixed with the boys much, or I was never in a group that mixed with the boys much. It definitely was a boy/girl thing. I don't think that's quite so bad now. I think there is a lot more mixing, because the kids like to do a lot of the same type of thing. It was very different then.

Even in the games in the playground, you'd get girls doing things like handstands or hopscotch and the boys would do all the running around making lots of noise. I can't remember sitting next to boys in the classroom, I think it was boy/girl splits in classrooms as well. I know now that they mix tables. Of course then it was long benches, nowadays it's all round tables so they can all be looking at each other.

Karen Clark

The boys used to raid the girls when they came out of cookery class. There never used to be many pastries because where the cookery class was, Miss Phillips used to take that, there were concrete stairs coming down right opposite 1A which was the class I was in.

We finished school at the same time as the girls came down these concrete stairs. Plink, plonk, you could hear them coming so we used to rush out and stand there. All the jam tarts, the mince pies and that, they all disappeared off the trays that they were taking home. One or two may have gone home but that's all.

Robert Pavely

They were all mixed classes. I don't remember anything adverse one way or the other. We were all in the class together and we did most of the same subjects. We did gardening and metalwork and they did cookery and needlework. Some of them learnt typing; I think they did have options of what they could take.

One or two girls did take metalwork. You were given a choice, I believe. But of course the accepted thing was to learn how to cook for the girls in those days and most of them went for that. We used to help them out with their cooking before they had a chance to take it home and show their parents. That was the normal sort of thing. They had netball teams and we had football teams. We used to go on bus trips to different schools and things like that. With a mixed school you always get the girlfriend/boyfriend syndrome, so everybody mixed in together.

Tony Stevens

UNIFORM

There wasn't a uniform when I was a pupil, I think there was when you got into the secondary school, but I'm not really sure. I know there was at the grammar school but I'm not really sure about the secondary school. There wasn't at primary. That was quite an expense for my parents when I started at the grammar school, because they had to buy all this uniform and everything.

Christine Hart

We usually wore grey flannel trousers, I remember that, long trousers mind you. I think we started there with long trousers which was really something then. We had blazers. Wartime again, there was no set school uniform as such, but we had a grey blazer and grey flannel trousers and we always had to wear a tie as well, that was more or less compulsory as I remember. We had a bag on the back of our bicycles and we'd take our things in there. We didn't have satchels.

Derek Bacon

I think I wore gym slips, but it wasn't uniforms, not then. Later on, it wasn't compulsory but it was suggested and they did go into red jumpers, red and grey I think it was.

Beryl Wade

There was no uniform. We used to wear a pinafore dress usually, or a blouse and skirt, jumper and skirt, mostly that. A lot of the girls who had sisters above them had gym slips and blouses, but we were never that well off so I had whatever was going, hand me downs, a lot of them. That didn't make me feel pretty, as long as I was warm and presentable.

Gwen Salmon

There was no uniform. But then, like all children, they make their own, don't they? They all like to have the same sort of things. There was no dress code, nor colour, nothing like that at all. I think secondary modern schools didn't, that was one of the things that distinguished them from grammar schools.

Hazel Smith

We had navy caps with HCS on the badge and navy blazers. That was the only uniform we had, no trousers or shorts or anything.

Percy Sizer

We didn't wear uniform, it was utility time. You were very lucky to get any clothes at all. We wore uniform when we went to the Sudbury school, that was the first time we had any touch with uniform. It was a job getting coupons to get the uniforms.

Jean Pavely

We had navy knickers and white T-shirts and that for games, but we didn't have uniform. I think it's a good thing you didn't really, because I don't think many parents could have afforded it. I can remember wearing my cousin's clothes because she was a couple of years older than me. When we first started the war hadn't been finished that long and a lot of people handed their clothes down. Everyone was in the same position, so nobody cared. I don't think we worried so much about what we wore then. There wasn't so much fashion, you've got to have this and you've got to have that like now.

Hilary Filben

We did have a school uniform at one stage. There was a Cangle tie; I think it was yellow and something, and grey skirts. But then later on, there wasn't any uniform at all and you'd wear your tank top and your lacy tights, two-tone skirts and your shirt with the pointy collars.

Jane Farrow

I had a draw string bag for my plimsolls for PE, but I don't think I had a satchel. I think I just had a carrier bag or any bag that was going. We never used to take books home like they do today as we never had homework.

Gwen Salmon

PREFECTS

There wasn't a head boy or head girl not at that school. Not until you got older really. At the secondary school there was, but not at primary. And there weren't really prefects, there were things like milk monitors and ink monitors, i.e. it was your turn that week to fill all the inkwells, you had to go to the cupboard and get the big can of ink and go round and fill them all up. Obviously the milk monitor took all the milk round to the different classes.

Christine Hart

We used to have the register monitors, the prefects, the headmistress's monitor and I went through all them which was rather nice. I was a prefect but they weren't called prefects then, I think they were called monitors. The register monitor had to go to the headmistress's office, knock on the door and wait quite a while before she'd say, come in. Then you just collected them. I don't remember having school secretaries, not then. We used to collect the registers, take them round to the teachers and then go and collect them later on in the day and taken them back to the headmistress. And it was quite important to do that. Ink monitors; we used to have someone who used to have to make sure the inkwells were filled up.

Beryl Wade

We had monitors for everything; pencil monitors, milk monitors, ink monitors, everything.

Hilary Filben

GANGS

There were little groups that we used to play with in the playground, but I don't think we had gangs as such. No, there wasn't gangs and there wasn't any trouble. We used to have one policemen there who used to keep track on us all in those days. He used to make sure we didn't misbehave ourselves in the streets, and of course the street lights went out at ten o'clock at night and we only had two in the street so nobody was ever around late.

Gladys Ely

When we got into the last year, there was a gang of the girls that was led by a girl called Pat Cliff and a lot of the time I was quite friendly with her, luckily. At one point, the boy who was the leader of the gang of boys rather liked me and that wasn't allowed because she was the leader, so he should have liked her. I had a bit of a rough time for a little while until he stopped liking me and liked somebody else. It all blew over after that.

Christine Hart

There were groups but not hostile groups. There'd be gangs for games, but no violence that I ever saw. I never saw any violence at Haverhill School at all, never. I never belonged to a gang. The only gang, the four of us was sufficient for us. I don't think there was any victimisation on any of the others either. That was how it was. It may have happened and I wasn't aware of it, but I can honestly say that I didn't encounter it at all.

Derek Bacon

There were gangs. It depended who you were friendly with that week. We used to call them gangs but they were friendly gangs. There was a young lad up here, he absolutely terrified me. He would hide behind a wall and jump out at me but that was terrible then. It wasn't the viciousness that it is now.

Beryl Wade

SCHOOL LUNCH

They didn't do school dinners when I was there. I suppose living so near in those days you just went home to dinner because the factory whistle used to go and things like that. We all went home for lunch and had to come back again in the afternoon.

Gladys Ely

I used to go home for lunch. They did do school dinners but I didn't have it. The canteen was at the top of the playground. To start with, I lived virtually just across the road from there. There was a small row of houses that went up by the side of the west end Congregational Church which was just across from the Cangle. We lived there until we were seven, and then we moved up to Duddery Hill, where my parents still live. So I always went home for lunch.

Christine Hart

We had a packed lunch for the first few months. After that, there were meals laid on at the town hall. I'm not sure how this all came about but they were certainly laid on during the war, not just for school children but for others as well. All those who stayed at school then were able to get a meal.

Derek Bacon

We used to go up to the town hall for our lunches, the children who came from a distance, which was at that time they called it a British restaurant. That was something they started during the war which people would go and buy a meal very cheaply, a good nutritional type meal. That's where we used to go up there for our lunch, that was before the days of school meals of course. The other, local children used to go home for lunch. Proper school lunches started after our time.

Val Gagen

The school dinners were up at the town hall and we used to have to come out of school, walk to the town hall and sit down and you were served by volunteers I assume, and they were free for the start. They were good meals and we used to have the meal and then come back to school and you had to report in. Some of the cutlery was a lot better than others, so we used to run up the town hall as fast as we could to get the best table. But we did used to have what I call good meals, which must have been difficult because rationing was on. The meals themselves were better than perhaps we could have had at home.

Gwen Salmon

We never had elaborate dinners. Mother used to make what we call meat puddings, some people call them steak and kidney puddings. We had them in the week. We'd have the pudding one day and some of the gravy and then she'd make another pastry the next day and that's when we had the meat. So she made it last two days.
Sainsbury's had a big place down Little Wratting, not big like it is now, that was only a small concern, but they killed pigs and that and one of their vans came round the town with all liver and sweetbreads and that all cut up. That was 4d a pound. Mother used to have on a Thursday, 2lb of that and do a baked hacelett in the oven. She used to put all vegetables and then on the top she used to put sliced potatoes. You never see that now in the butcher's shop, the pig's curtain, it was like lace. She used to get a bit of that and put it over the top and that used to bake up crispy, it was lovely. We had onion pudding with that on a Thursday and potatoes.
We never knew what custard was. I never had custard till I went in the forces. I never had butter. All we had was margarine. If we had bread and jam, we weren't allowed margarine on the bread, we used to have the bread and jam. We never had all these fancy things like people get now. We were brought up plain, but my mother gave us a good dinner. Sometimes, when the rhubarb was ready, she'd cook up a big basin of that and we'd all have some in a little dish with a piece of bread to dip in. We thought we were kings and queens. We only had a whole boiled egg once a year and that was Easter Sunday. At other times of the year, sometimes mother would do us mashed potatoes and peas or whatever there was, and we had half a fried egg. She couldn't afford to give us a whole one.
When my uncle was a fish merchant she used to buy herrings from uncle but we only had a half of one each with mashed potatoes. We never had a rice pudding like I have now. Mum used to boil it in a bag and we had jam on it. But we weren't starved, we never went about hungry. We were happy and contented and healthy. We never had the complaints like they do now.

Percy Sizer

We used to have our meal at lunchtime. There were no school meals and children didn't take sandwiches. We were expected to go home for our meal from 12 to 1.30. When we went to Sudbury we had school dinners. Gurteen's factory worked until 6 o'clock and we would have our tea when your dad came home. You all ate together, never in relays.

Diane Basham

I remember having my school meals there. I don't think they were very nice, I didn't enjoy those very much. We used to have to eat it. They used to be very strict and they used to try and make you clear up your food. We could have seconds if we wanted, but not many people did, I don't think. If you were first sitting, you used to be really pleased because you got the choice of everything. Third was dreadful, you just got what the others left, what they didn't want.

Hilary Filben

I didn't go home for lunch. When we first went there, when we came out of class we all used to make our way up to the town hall and all trestle tables were set out. A year or two after that they built a new canteen at the back of the school.
Food was still on ration at that of course. You could get a better meal at school for two and sixpence a week than you could at home. Although the war finished in 1945 rationing went on into the '50's.

Tony Stevens

My mum was a dinner lady at the Cangle, and my grandma was also a dinner lady, so we had two Mrs Agers as dinner ladies. When it came to Christmas school dinners, they'd be a little tradition of sometimes in the Christmas pudding there'd be a sixpence. But if you sat on my table, you would definitely get a sixpence in your Christmas pudding, it was magic.
I don't think I enjoyed the school dinners very much. I seem to remember telling one teacher that I wasn't on school dinner. She went and checked with my brother who then told her that I was.

Jane Farrow

I can't remember people having packed lunches very much. I remember one girl who used to live right at the top of the Chalkstone estate, and she used to walk home to dinner, which must have been getting on for a mile, I should think to her house, and then about a mile back again, after dinner, so she would have walked about four miles a day, getting to school and going back for dinner, getting back from dinner and then walking home again after school.

Geoffrey Ship

MILK

We had school milk in 1/3 pint bottles which were brought round in a crate with a straw. It tasted OK but the trouble was in the summer it was warm because it just came in the crate and there it stood until you had it at break, so it wasn't very nice in the summertime. In the winter of course it was absolutely freezing. But it didn't put me off milk, I still like milk now.

Christine Hart

We used to have little tiny bottles. There was a little hole in the lid which you would put the straw in, and if you had two and you collected the tops and washed them you could make little bobbles with the wool, for your hats and things. You never wasted anything you see. This makes you feel very old you know.

Gwen Salmon

We never used to have school milk. The poorer class people used to get some of this cod liver oil. It used to be issued free, so many tins a month. It was given to them at the school. Their parents had to go down and collect it.

Harold Sozer

Milkman near Cangle school *From a collection of old postcards*

We did get a little bottle of milk, free milk. Special little bottles for schools. Cardboard top, you pushed the middle in. The middle bit was perforated, you pushed it in and then put your straw in. I remember that.

Cyril Nunn

I didn't like milk to drink, especially warm milk, and it used to take me all the playtime to drink my milk. When we were infants and juniors they had cardboard tops with a punched hole in the middle, and you also had a straw. In the junior school we used to wash these tops, and one Christmas we used these to make a mobile, which I think was with Mrs Beer. We were allowed to take these mobiles home when the Christmas holidays arrived.

Diane Basham

They used to put the milk on the stone floors in the lobbies because that would keep it as cool as possible. I hated that hot milk. Every child was supposed to drink it and it was ages before I could persuade my mother to write a note and say I ought not to have it. I was always a fat little girl but I suppose she thought that was good for me.

Jean Pavely

In the wintertime we used to go up to the metalwork room and stand the bottles on the boiler to warm up, or melt the ice as it was, because the little foil tops on the bottles had risen up about an inch where the ice had pushed them up.

Hilary Filben

My main memories of the school seem to be around being a milk monitor. We used to have to deliver milk to all the classrooms. The couple of people I got friendly with must have been doing it. We used to have to take the milk crates round so that every class had its third of a pint of milk. It sounds really old now, it sounds like something your grandfather would have said. The reward for that really is that you could drink as much milk as you wanted at the end, with whatever was left. I don't know that I particularly liked it but you still drunk it anyway. I don't particularly like milk now.

Gerry Kiernan

SPECIAL MEMORIES

I have so many good memories. I liked most of what when on at the school. It's a very narrow existence in a village school. Even just going to Haverhill was really something for us, all the different subjects that we could get involved with. The swimming and all these other activities that went on were brilliant. I suppose going there, my parents were rather good to me because after that they got me an engineering apprenticeship which was good, so that put me in good stead from there. It gave me a good start and things worked out quite well.

Derek Bacon

Class 3 1930 *History Group*

To be honest, I can't really remember any unhappy moments at school. I loved school. I wasn't very good at art, but we didn't do a lot of that. Sports days, I wasn't all that wrapped up in because the only thing I could do really was netball, apart from swimming. I couldn't sing, I'm not a singer.

Beryl Wade

The winters seemed colder than they are now. I can remember snow drifts and all sorts of things, wrapping up. I remember the teacher, the children used to take the mickey because when you cycle obviously you want lots of clothes on and they used to take the mickey. I remember the teacher once, he had me out the front and I'd thought I'd done something wrong. But she said, this young girl has biked from Thurlow and she was here on time; you live across the road and you were late. I was really relieved, I really thought I was in trouble. I did that until I left school but never thought a lot of it. We used to have the dentist come in a caravan in the playground and when he turned up we all used to shake.
We had one teacher collapse and die at school, I can remember, that was a sad moment because we all liked her. Apart from that, I can't remember much sadness, we always used to have a laugh most of the time amongst ourselves. A very pleasant time, I thought.

Gwen Salmon

I had a very nasty mishap one day. I can remember it now. I was in Mr Smith's class.

I was the second one from the top, because he did two classes: standard 6 and standard 7 and I was in standard 6. On a Thursday morning we had spelling lessons at 11 o'clock. I can see myself now where I sat. I got up to do some spelling and the lad the other side of me, he had one of those knives which had one blade. It used to file down, they were a penny and you used to get them in the market. Well, he'd put that down where I was going to sit, but he didn't think I was going to sit down so quick and I sat down on it. It just missed the heart of one of my privates. I screamed out and I ran all the way home with this knife sticking in me. The caretaker, Mr Scrivener, had to come right up to my house and take it out and do it up. I had to take a cushion for three weeks to sit on at school because I didn't want to stay home from school. The doctor said I was a very lucky fellow. The boy got moved out of the class.

Percy Sizer

Another thing I remember is that we had a tuck shop. It wasn't particularly a shop but the stock was kept up some sort of rickety stairway in a little room. We took it in turns to be tuck monitors, I remember doing that one day. Mars bars were 21/2p, I think, or 5p and crisps were 21/2p, one of the two. That's how cheap they were. They were about the same price as in the shops. I remember there had been a Budget and the price of crisps and all the other tuck things had come down a bit and I thought it was wonderful, I thought the Budgets were great.

Julie Smith

I recollect that the library was run out of Mr Williams' classroom at the Cangle. I can remember stamping the tickets and putting them in a little pocket at the front of the book. It must have been in the war, because I can't think where the library was run from before. Afterwards, it was in a room in the town hall. Anybody could come in and use the library.
We used to have Scouts and the Cubs. Mr Underwood was Scout leader. And Mr Williams was the ATC man. They used to run the ATC from there. All the youth clubs used to have to be in the school because that was the only thing available. The Guides used to meet in the West end schoolroom and the Brownies. It was the evacuees that introduced Brownies into the town. One of the leaders of the evacuees was a Guider and they brought the Brownies with them. I don't know about the Scouts. The only room that was available was that middle room where everything happened. It was used every night of the week for something. The youth club used to have it on Friday nights. Mr Underwood and Miss Castle used to run this youth club. She always used to say that you were never allowed to refuse a lad. If a lad comes and asks a girl to dance, she's got to do it and say yes.

Jean Pavely

I remember when there was a flood and the school got flooded out. It would be about 1958 and all the parents had to go and scrub the school out. You see, the river runs underneath the school. It was that high up Max's windows, the hairdresser's at the bottom of this road.

The front page of the Daily Mirror at the time had got a policeman walking along the bottom of Corn Road up to his waist in water.

Albert Smith used to keep the pub The Plough, he was a carpenter by trade. His wheelbarrow finished up down at the other end of town.

When the sun came out, you could see all the windows reflected in the water. It wasn't just a little bit of pond, it had a current on it. It was going at a fair rate of knots, much more than usual round here. The river was really running. We'd had a lot of rain. Days and days of rain.

The pressure of the water was such that it was forcing water up the hill something like 100 feet through the water system which should have been draining the other way. There was sufficient force on it to lift a manhole cover, a little square one. It must have come up all through the toilets and everything.

It started raining on the Saturday dinnertime. It rained all Saturday afternoon and evening, Sunday all day and finished on Monday and that's when the floods were out, Monday morning. I was waiting for the lorry to pick me out here to go to a show and it didn't turn up. I found out in the end, the water was halfway up the wheels in the yard.

Robert & Jean Pavely

Floods 1958 *Ken Williams*

Maureen Argent was one of my best friends. Her father had a farm which was actually right in the town. Down at the bottom of the recreation ground there's an old people's home called Place Farm and that's where it was, the farm was there. The farmhouse was there and there was a yard behind it with pigs there and barns. His main fields weren't in the town, obviously, but the actual farmhouse and his farmyard were in the town. There were a couple of paddocks behind there where they had horses and things. I was chased by a pig in that yard once, I've got a scar on my knee because of it. I went round to Maureen's one day during the holidays and I went in through the gate and a sow had got loose and it was running around the yard. They said to me "keep out the way, keep out the way", and it chased me and I fell over on the gravel. I got all this gravel in my knee and I've still got the scar to this day. They caught the pig, luckily. She used to have a huge Old English Sheepdog which was the smelliest dog I've ever seen. Every time I went round to the house it used to jump up to greet me and put its paws on my shoulders. It was as tall as I was and it was just disgusting. I don't know they could live with it, it smelt really awful.

I used to go round her house quite a lot and she had a record player, a Dancette. I had one eventually as well, but she had one before I did because her father was a farmer so she was better off than me. We used to have records; we didn't have very many because we couldn't afford very many. We were very fond of Dickie Valentine. We used to talk about joining his fan club.

Christine Hart

I can't remember much about the nursery apart from one day I went without any knickers on, because I got myself dressed and just forgot.

I can remember us having to do, we each had a room to do in a house, we made a house out of boxes and we had to go into groups and make, I think I had the bedroom to do with friends. We made all little curtains and beds and things like that. Papier maché was a big thing in that year, papier maché everything.

I can remember my friend used to stack the papers. I don't know why we kept the papers at that point. I think you got a certain amount per ton and we got money for it, I'm not sure. It was at the bottom of our classroom. One day the bulb blew and fell onto the papers and they caught alight and started a fire, which was quite scary. So obviously that was a proper drill where they actually came and put something out. They said they knew we would all get out OK because you did so well in the practices anyway.

The only school play I can ever remember being in, it was called The Little Fir Tree and I was playing the mother. I had to knit and for the life of me could not knit so I just had to sit there clicking the knitting needles together so that it sounded like I was knitting.

Jane Duffy

I can remember an occasion when Miss Martin stuck a dummy into Colin's mouth because he was crying all the time. I remember we had slates, although we didn't do sums or anything, just pictures. They must have been leftovers. I can remember coloured bricks and I wanted to build a house, a real house. I got upset because I couldn't find enough bricks to make a house. The other thing I remember is, in the playground at the front of the Cangle, we were dancing round the conker tree to "Rock Around The Clock".

Peter Isaacs

When you were in a lower class, every week on a Friday you were given a ticket. On that ticket it used to say "always clean, hands, legs, face" and you had that ticket to take home. If you didn't take that ticket home your parents would want to know why you hadn't got a ticket. You'd been playing about somewhere on the way to school and messed yourself up.

A chap used to come there with shoes for those who couldn't afford it. Some children didn't have shoes. Some parents used to send their children in an old pair to get a new pair of shoes. The shoes were really stiff.

Harold Sozer

The Friday before the war broke out, I was over at my friend's with my sister. Unbeknown to us, my mother had had a boy on the Wednesday, August 30th, and this particular day my dad came over with Archie Smith, Archie had a car, and brought us home because war was imminent. As we got out of the car to go up to where we lived, Mrs Offord, her husband was inspector wasn't he, she said, have you got that baby in that case? My dad said she would open her mouth! That was the Friday and then Sunday war was declared. I can remember that day as if it were yesterday.

There was one time when there was a violent thunderstorm and we were all in assembly; because we always had to have assembly every morning, regular as anything. We used to have to learn a different hymn every little while for assembly. Miss Potter told us all that God was moving his furniture about. I can remember going home and saying to my mother, "that's not true, is it?".

Jean Pavely

We had a girl called Heather and she used to drink the ink. I don't know what it was, she just liked ink. We used to go to our inkwells and say, "the ink's run out again" and everybody used to say, "Heather!". She used to say, "it's not me" and she had this big blue ring round her mouth, so we knew it was.

There was a little shop which now is the double glazing shop, it used to be a little white sweet shop. We always used to go in there before school. We weren't really allowed to eat in school but we did. We used to lift the desks up and have something to eat. A teacher caught me eating an apple once. He was one of my favourite teachers, actually, but he caught me eating this apple and he made me stand out in the front of the class and finish that apple in front of everybody. I went off the apple after that.

Hilary Filben

Opposite the school, the small thatched shop (now the double glazing shop) sold, amongst other goods, Tizer and Corona drinks, which we would leave school in playtime, against the rules, to buy a bottle which two or three shared. During the following lessons, a loud 'burp' or two was heard from different areas of the room accompanied by muffled titters. Some teachers tried to find the culprits, but others tried to ignore what were some rude manners.
Ellis Bakery was also visited during the dinner the break and a bread roll secreted in a jacket pocket. During the class a hand would pull off a bit of bread and nibble without being caught, not that anyone was hungry.

Roy Brazier

Sweetshop, Withersfield Road c1960 *History Group*

One of the treats we used to have was watching the white mice in cages at school. In turn, we were allowed to bring the mice home for the weekend, and when we took them back there were more mice than what we brought home. They had a litter during the weekend, so mother came with me and explained all that.
The headmaster, Mr Bartholomew, was a bit jokey. Well, in the class there was Neville Pearson who was a farmer's son. There was a bit read out of a story somewhere, "the cock crowed on dunghill" and this Neville Pearson said, "Please sir, what is a dunghill?" He said, "You a farmer's son and you don't know what a dunghill is?" Of course, the rest of the class soon told him.

Robert Pavely

There was a dinner lady called Mrs Swan. She was very sweet and she had white hair. I can remember spotting these pennies the other side of the railings. They weren't mine, but I told her they were and I asked if I could go and get them, because you weren't allowed outside. So she said yes I could. So we pootled outside and later on I probably spent them in White Shop. The sweet shop opposite was always called the White Shop. I always got my pennies and spent them at the White Shop. The husband

and wife who ran that, I always remember him being very tall and thin and she was very short and fat, total opposites.
I remember Mr Roy, he was my form teacher. He was a super teacher, absolutely brilliant. I used to have a lisp. Two of us in the class had a lisp and we used to go to speech therapy. We used to go somewhere in the school up the stairs in a little room, I couldn't tell you where it was. The pair of us used to go, quite meekly, and we didn't even know we had lisps, we had no idea that we spoke peculiar to everybody else. We had to do this little rhyme. He'd always ask us what we did when we came back, he was quite interested. We'd say we had to practice a rhyme and he'd say, well can you tell it to the class? And we'd say no, no, we couldn't tell it to the class, because we're far too shy. We did in fact tell the class eventually, but we said we'd stand behind the blackboard, because it was a blackboard that was on wheels and pulled out. You can imagine these scrawny little legs and grey socks rolled down to your ankles and we would be saying, "A baby sardine saw its first submarine. It was scared as it looked through the peephole. 'Come, come, come, come', said the sardine's mum, 'it is only a tin full of people'." And it took us ages to say it. That was our speech therapy, in 1965 or whatever it was.

Jane Farrow

We had a production one year and, I can't remember the name of my class teacher at the time, but I basically went through my whole school year with another girl called Kerry Jane Davis. We were in the same class for all our school life. There's always somebody in your class who is the best at everything, the reading and she'd always get ten out of ten for the spellings and have more red stars and more silver stars. If you had ten red stars you'd get a silver star. And we had to read for these parts. We were going to do The Owl and the Pussycat at the town hall. Mr Danes, who was really keen on dramatics and productions, was brilliant at getting us to project our voices. You probably wouldn't tell it now, but it was very good. We had to read for these parts and I was going to go for the pussycat and Kerry went for the pussycat as well. I was thinking, I'm not going to get this. We both had a reading. I think it must have been a fairly close decision, but they said yes, I could be the pussycat.
Then of course you had to have the costume. This means that I had to be in black. Well, we had nothing black. I had no black tights, no black jumper. So mum went next door and Margaret next door had a black jumper. She probably shrunk it in the wash or something, but that fitted me, and somebody had some black tights. I can remember having this black tail stuffed, it must have looked quite hideous.
I can't remember who was the owl, but we had the pea-green boat on the stage and we had the bags of money. We had to lift it up at the right place. I'm sure Kevin Cuffly was the pig with the ring through his nose. There was the island scene with the trees, and the

trees were people, the other children and they were made out tubes of brown sugar paper with the leaves all round. The only thing is, at the back of the town hall, when you come up the steps, they are so steep, you can't actually get up them in a tube of brown paper. I can remember Mr Kiddingback, I think, who was the deputy head at one stage, he was lifting trees up the back stage onto the main stage. I can remember doing that and I thought that was wonderful. It was probably the first time I'd ever spoken in public.

Jane Farrow

Cangle entertains 1966 *Newspaper cutting*

When I was about 6 or 7 my mum and dad bought me a watch for my birthday and I learned how to tell the time and I think I was the only boy in the class who could tell the time and I remember the teacher used to keep asking me, about every half an hour, Geoffrey, can you tell everybody what the time is. That made me feel very proud as well, because I thought I could do something that nobody else could do, so I can remember looking at my brand new watch and telling everybody the time when they asked me.

We got to take our cycling proficiency test and we got a certificate and a badge for that, which I've still got at home and I found it ever so hard because there was one bit where you had to make your bike go in and out of some tin cans and I couldn't do that, and the policeman who tested us was very kind, he kept moving the tin cans further and further apart so we could get in and out of them. Everybody else used to find that quite easy but I found it quite hard.

The teacher used to write nice things in your book, and have a word with your mum and dad sometimes when they used to come and pick you up from school, she used to say that Geoffrey had worked hard today or something like that, which was quite nice. And it would get on the school report at the end of the year, that you'd worked hard. We used to get stars, but they weren't the ones that you peel off and stick in now, they were ones you had to lick and the gum on the back wasn't very good so they often used to fall out of your book.

Geoffrey Ship

Our two Caretakers, by the way, served as pall-bearers to the local undertaker as and when required, so could often be seen in their "seen-better-days" black pin-stripes, complete with plastic clip-on ties, returning to school in the late afternoon to do their after-school duties. Quite a bizarre sight!

Alan Haigh

THE WAR

There was always lots of activities in the school, despite it being the war. We used to have a youth club every Friday night run by some of the staff at school and the lessons were normal lessons for a normal school. Then of course we were combined with the Page Green School that came from Tottenham which were evacuated to Haverhill, so we were combined with the teachers. They intermixed with the teachers of the old Haverhill school. We still used to have all normal things go on there, like a very good netball team and a very good drama class. We put on plays, The Tempest and Midsummer Night's Dream, but they used to have to go on at the town hall because we never had a proper stage and things, not like schools have now.
My uncle was friendly with the chap in the Black Horse pub, so when the siren went we used to go down in their cellar and I can remember running down there one day and the plane came over and was machine gunning across the rec. I think there was a couple of times when bombs dropped in Haverhill, but mainly they were over Haverhill before they knew they were there really because we were only a tiny little place in a hollow. The houses never went no further than Burton End, Chainey Pieces and just up the top of Mill Hill and I can remember going up there and when the first raids on London, when London was caught alight I can remember standing right up on the top there and you could see all the orange glow in the sky over London then.
I don't think we were ever really frightened about it, because you weren't told so much in those days because there was no television or any local papers and of course the other papers couldn't print very much because they were censored on what they were allowed to say. We just carried on a normal life.

Gladys Ely

We had gas masks; whether we took them to school I can't remember. I think after the first year or two years no-one really bothered with gas masks so much then. The only thing you remember well about the war is if an aeroplane had crashed or a bomb had fallen somewhere, you used to go out of curiosity to see what it was all about. We had lots of aircraft crashed here.
The only time I was frightened was when I saw a Sterling aircraft crash within about 100 yards from where I was, but I wasn't frightened of the war. I was frightened at the beginning of the war when we had to go and be measured for gas masks. The other thing which is very dear to me, and probably still is, that were we going to have enough to eat? Although we only had a few rations, I don't ever remember going hungry really at all.

Derek Bacon

During the war we were not able to do certain things. Science finished because you couldn't get different things, I can't remember what now. We had cookery lessons, we had dried eggs, soya flour and all that sort of thing because you couldn't get fresh eggs. Dreadful things, but we ate them!

We had a lot of evacuees here from London that came down. When you're young you don't realise why they were there, but when you get older you realise why. They're talking about small classes now, but we used to have 40 in a class in those days, easily. But we never used to complain. We still all learnt; chanting our tables like they're going to do again. I have happy memories of the Cangle.

VJ Day, Street party 1945 *History Group*

My father was in the Forces and my mother used to get ten shillings a week. Well, that wasn't a lot even in those days, so there wasn't a lot left over for sweets. But you could get them on ration, on your coupon. You had to give coupons up for everything, or have your ration book marked. But there were sweets to be hand and there used to be a little shop just along from Withersby Road, a Mrs Sayers her name was, a lovely lady. I don't know how she did it, but she always used to have some that were three for a penny, off ration. A certain amount and when they were gone they were gone. I can remember getting three little sticks of toffee for a penny and we thought that was wonderful, off the ration. Something you felt that you were having for free, or nearly free.

We had to have a gas mask and you had to be tested for this gas mask every now and again. I can remember they brought a big van and we had to sit in this van, I suppose about ten of us, five each side. And they would feed the tear gas in, to see if your gas mask fitted. I can remember we were all a bit nervous. They said they wouldn't open the door up, that they would know if it was on purpose. I was fine but there was one girl, I can remember, that she yelled and her eyes were all red. But that was the test should there have been a gas attack, that your gas mask was right. Because we never went anywhere without your gas mask. If we went up the playing fields you always had to take your gas mask. Everywhere you went. You were told off about it if you hadn't got it, they used to check you. There used to be a cardboard box with a bit of string on and it used to go everywhere. I remember my uncle bought me one in the shape of the gas mask, I thought that was wonderful, without this cardboard box. That was something we had to live with.

Sometimes the teacher would announce that someone wasn't in today because they'd lost their father, brother, uncle or whatever, that was rather sad. Being a small community, we knew who they were, as opposed to somebody who was just a name and that was a bit sad.

Gwen Salmon

The war broke out when we were five, so things were short and on rations.
When the sirens went I can remember going into this very dark place within the school, and the lighting wasn't very powerful. This was the cloakroom area with our gas masks which we used to take to school with us. Obviously they were issued at the beginning of the war and I can remember walking alone with this little box round our neck. We used to have gas mask drill where they used to have us put them on. They were awful and they had this awful smell about them.
I remember one bomb landing one night, when my dad was on Air Raid Protection duty. They used to have concrete shelters, and there was one on the recreation ground in Haverhill where my dad went. They were basically there to help the people who had perhaps been bombed. There were cornfields on both sides of us, and this particular night one dropped in this field and I can remember being very frightened. I cannot remember what age I was but it was before I was eleven.
Then there were doodlebugs that came over in 1944, and I can remember one summer night watching this doodlebug go over, which were pilotless. You heard them and then suddenly they just stopped and you knew it was coming down. It went over and dropped in open countryside between Haverhill and Withersfield.
I remember the victory celebrations we had, but again we were only eleven.
The war finished on V.E. Day, May 8th 1945, and August 15th was V.J. Day. I remember these dates because V.J. Day was the day before mum's birthday.
I remember we had celebrations and that V.J. Day was during the school holidays. There were flags out, but that is all I can remember.
I can remember during the wartime we had a market day on Friday opposite the Post Office, and there was a flower stall that I used to queue up at to get 1/2lb of tomatoes. You could queue for up to 2 hours and then you might not get any as they might have sold out. I can also remember queuing up after the war for oranges and bananas.
During the war we ate rabbit, there wasn't anything else. You had sausages made by the butchers which weren't rationed, and were only made at the weekends. I didn't like sausages because in those days they had big bits of gristle in them. They were really meaty in fact, not like they are now.
You reared chicken and killed your own. We had some and had a few eggs. When you had surplus eggs my mother would out them in an icing glass to preserve them. I can remember cooking with dried egg yolk, and the scrabbled egg and omelette was OK using this.

Diane Basham

You reconstituted dried egg with water. In fact, my only school prize from Sudbury, which was a practical housekeeping book, had recipes which had dried egg in them. We used go into the harvest fields a lot, the harvest fields were very close then. I was told that I could talk to the Italian prisoners of war but I mustn't talk to the Germans. I don't know why. The Italian prisoners were quite nice. They couldn't speak English much, but it was the regular thing for all the children to go. When you got to the last part of the field, the binder goes round and round and round and gradually the amount of corn that's left gets smaller and smaller, then you surround it and all the boys have got cudgels or some sort of stick. When the rabbits came out you'd hit them over the head, take them home and mum used to have rabbit pie.

I can remember being taken to the top of the field to see the gliders leave for D-Day. They assembled somewhere over here. When you looked at them, it seemed odd because the plane that was pulling the glider always seemed lower than the glider that it was pulling.

Jean Pavely

I know when the air-raid siren went we used to get up in the middle of the night and go down to my aunt's, who lived not many yards away, and go down her cellar. But after a time we became quite blasé about it I suppose. Youngsters followed their parents so we didn't think we were in any danger. We weren't really threatened, were we?

We didn't have any bombs, well there might have been an odd one. Straddishall was an airbase and also Ridgewell was the American base, wasn't it?

Muriel Moore

I can remember the Battle of Britain. Over the top here there were all Spitfires and German planes dive-bombing each other and intercepting each other. We had a dug-out in the back garden which my father and Mr Gibbs made between them. It used to take the twelve of us in this dug-out.

The bottom of our garden now is all the Downs estate but years ago it was all chickens and pigs places and allotments. The cannon shells were falling on the galvanised roofs of those pigs places like hailstones rattling on a piece of glass, I can hear them now. My grandmother didn't want to go and have her breakfast. She came down there with her breakfast and we said, "Come on in, you'll get killed".

Robert Pavely

CHRISTMAS

Everywhere was decorated at Christmas. We always used to make paper chains and decorate the school. I don't remember nativity plays, but we must have done them. I remember that mainly in Mrs Corkindale's class, because I was older then.

Christine Hart

I remember we used to decorate the classes up with the paper chains we used to sit and make in those days, but I can't remember an awful lot. I suppose because the war was on things were restricted a lot more than they would have been.

Gladys Ely

We used to do the little plays at Christmas, but it was always a little religious play, mostly the nativity. I don't think it was done by classes, it was done en block of the school. The parents used to come and watch us. When I was working at the school, it was given to me to organise the Christmas parties with the help of the other ancillaries plus the help of the parents. We used to go and shop at the cash and carry. The year when we had over a thousand pupils, we made jellies and sandwiches and all that sort of thing. We gave them a really good do. It took us all day every day for about a week. They didn't have it all at once, not when I worked there. Certain days were certain years. They used to do some very nice Christmas plays then. Every year had a different day and the parents came as well. When I was a child at school it was unheard for parents to come into the school. If a parent came into the school it was either after the headmistress or the teacher or something like that. But when I worked there, they came in to help, much appreciated help.

Beryl Wade

We had a Christmas party, but not from the school. The soldiers used to give us a Christmas party at the town hall and the London Irish were down here, with the green feather. They used to march us up with the pipe band, I used to think it was wonderful. We used to have everything, jelly and the lot. They must have obviously saved up and given us this from that and we thought that was really wonderful. I can remember that was the highlight really.
We had Christmas nativity plays, where you played an angel or whatever with the school. I was an angel once, and then a mother, Joseph's mother or something. I didn't like it, I don't like being in the limelight, I like behind the scene work far better. I'm still a bit like that, I don't like to be at the forefront of anything. I'm self-conscious rather than shy I think. My job was meeting the public all the time, but I'm alright with that. Anything social, I'm rather a home bird in that respect. But I did have some good years there.

Gwen Salmon

At Christmas I was in nativity plays; I was in The Little Fir Tree and then I went on to being in the choir or playing the recorder or what have you. It was always really good fun where your mums and dads came to watch you. There were so many showings throughout the week. I think you did two or three of the same showing so that all the parents could come. I can remember all the seats being laid out and you just looked for your mum and she always seemed to be in the back.

Jane Duffy

At Christmas time, when we were smaller, we used to make paper chains and lanterns out of what your mother used to have left over from paper in the room. The lanterns were made out of scraps of wallpaper, and we brought these home when we knocked off for Christmas.

Percy Sizer

At Christmas you just had Christmas Day, Boxing Day and you might get one day extra and then you were back at school again. There was no New Year's Day or anything like that then. It was a very short holiday. And we only had four weeks in the summer. At Easter, we had Good Friday and Easter Monday and then back to school again. Not like they do now. We never had a half term to forget what we'd learned.

Harold Sozer

Christmas was a very happy time and very family orientated as far as I was concerned, probably because we were a large family with brothers and sisters and all the cousins and so on. They came back to Haverhill for Christmas. There wasn't any decorations as such, just paper chains they still have today.
We didn't have many sweets, but what sweets there were, they were wrapped with this foil around them, and we used to save all the coloured foil. We used to gather wheat and oats and each little kernel we would turn this foil round and this made a very attractive decoration.

Diane Basham

The London Irish regiment was stationed here. They had a wolfhound and a piped band and they wore kilts, but not Scottish kilts, they were a tan colour. They took all the infants from the Cangle School up to the town hall, which is now called the Arts Centre, for a Christmas party. We all had to march up the street behind this band. Mother said that when she came to fetch me home, there was me sitting on the knee of one of these Irish bandsman, and Dorothy Carr sitting one of the other's. She said those men were having the time of their lives because they hadn't got their families.

Jean Pavely

We had a big Christmas tree in the hall and we sang carols and that sort of thing. We bought the teachers presents. We did carol concerts and plays for the parents. There was lots of snow, we used to have a lot of snow in those days. I remember going to school and throwing snowballs and having snowball fights.

Hilary Filben

One thing I do remember about Christmas is that we had ice cream. We used to get those little blocks of ice cream rolled up in paper and that was a real treat. We never had drinks; the only time you could have a drink was if you pretended you had something stuck in your throat and you'd get a glass of water.

Julie Smith

We had a film show for one Christmas, I can't remember what year. It was Wizard of Oz and it was the first I'd seen Wizard of Oz. It was on a ciné camera type thing on a big screen in the dining room. I can still remember the gasp when it turned from black and white to colour. That was our Christmas treat.

Karen Clark

The School 1975 *History Group*

We always had a Christmas party, held in the town hall. There was always a big run-up to the Christmas party. Of course, when you're 14/15 you're always trying to persuade some young lady to be your partner for that night. We came out of school and the ones that lived in Haverhill used to go home and put their smart things on and the rest of us used to have to stay as we were. We just used to go to school looking a bit smarter that day. They used to be quite good parties because they always taught dancing at school. They used to work that in just before the party so there was no excuse for anybody who couldn't dance. It used to be quite amusing sometimes.

Tony Stevens

To celebrate Christmas, we would always watch the Wizard of Oz which I seem to remember was black and white. I know it's a colour film and it starts black and white, so maybe that's why I remember it. But it was always the Wizard of Oz and I think you had an apple and/or an orange. I can't remember anything spectacular really but it was the same film. You could never see it because there'd be about a hundred of you in the canteen. And it was always crackly and you could never hear it properly either.

Jane Farrow

OUTINGS

The Co-op used to give us a treat in August and we used to have Sunday School treats round-about 15 July, St Swithin's time. We were lucky if we had a fine day, really, on the Wednesday. We all marched through the town and went down to the Hamlet Croft. We all split up then in the different Sunday Schools and we had games and that. Then you used to come back to your own place at teatime. They used to give us a tea and then we went back again at night to finish the games and all that off.
The Co-op treat was lovely because we used to march through the town then. They had all competitions down there, advertising their polishes etc. The girls had to clean spoons with the CWS Brasso stuff. The boys used to go in and clean shoes. They were terrible. We used to use the CWS shoe polish and they would give us your brushes and everything. Then we all had to sit down on planks outside this big marquee and the ladies came round with the big mugs. They brought the tea round in watering cans, new ones that had never been used, and they filled your mugs up. Then they came round with linen baskets with all the sandwiches in. Then they came round with all the cake and all things like that.

Percy Sizer

We went to Ely and we went on a boat on the canal. I went to Grimes graves with the school on the same day, I think. I think it was an annual thing for the oldest children.

Gerry Kiernan

We went on a school trip to a place called Grimes Graves, it's near Thetford Forest and it's a place where Stone Age people used to dig in the ground to get flints to make flint axes with and you can still go down into the tunnels that Stone Age people dug to get the flints out, because the flints that are buried deep in the ground, they make better axes than the ones that are on top of the ground, so they used to dig a mine and we were allowed to go down. You went down a rope ladder that swung backwards and forwards, we were all a bit scared of it, and when we got down there we were allowed to crawl in all the tunnels where they used to dig out the flints, and that was really good, thinking that people had crawled in those same tunnels thousands of years ago and I was crawling in them as well. And the tunnels were so small that once you got in, you couldn't turn round, so you had to come out of them backwards and I remember there was a boy called John Whybrow who was very small and he wriggled a long, long way into the tunnel and then he couldn't turn round to come out and then all the teachers and almost all the other children were too big to go in and get him because he was the smallest boy in the class, and I think we had to pull him out by his legs in the end. That was the best trip I can remember.

Geoffrey Ship

TEACHERS STORIES

As a teacher coming and being young and one of the few females, you more or less did what you were told, shall we say. Therefore it was PE and games for girls and a bit of needlework and Maths and English was my own class. You didn't come in with your subject, you came in and accepted your timetable and that was it. Of course the school playing field was at Wratting Road, and so three afternoons a week in the summer we trailed all the way up there. On Wednesdays it was twice in the afternoon. You brought one lot straight after lunch and the others. You never stayed for the whole afternoon, you came back for afternoon break and took another lot. Outdoor PE was done on that sloping playground, which was challenging to say the least.

Being one of the female staff at Christmas, the four of us spent two or three evenings up in the cookery room making great bowls of jelly. We made it in these big bowls that were cream on the outside and white on the inside, and I think the parents would donate these jellies and we would start off by sorting all the packets into all the same colours. Then you sorted the colours into flavours and proceeded from there to make these jellies, and for the actual party they all used to sit down and they had sandwiches, cakes and jellies. I suppose they must have been those long trestle tables that belonged to the Town Hall. I can just remember the chaos when they'd all finished eating, all these tables and chairs were moved away and the drugget was rolled up off the floor so they could dance or play games. But the business of having all these children and moving all the furniture, it was quite something. This was in two sessions with the lower two years having theirs on one night and then the older ones on the other night.

It was fun. The older girls all made Christmas cakes in the domestic science room, so if you went up into the room at the end of Christmas term there would be all these little fruitcakes. They used to ice them and take them home. I think it was a good thing to do. They still collect their dinner money, which used to be the bane of my life on Monday mornings. We had all the village children and so many of them stayed for lunch, and on Friday afternoon you would get the credits back if they had been absent. The secretary came round and actually brought the money back to the class teacher. If the child was still away on the Friday you had to look after it until they came back. There was a lot of that sort of admin that went on, but it seemed to slot into the day somehow. I invigilated the 11+ on a couple of occasions, because the invigilators had to be people who hadn't got children who were likely to take it within a certain time, that was one of the rules.

The pupils sat the 11+ in one of the classrooms in the upper part of the school. They would come in for the day and all the rest had the day off. Gordon Graham took his 11+ the first year that I was here, that's Mr Graham the chemist who's now retired. I remember because Mr Graham was one of the school governors and we'd got his son sitting there doing the 11+.

The pupils were quite tense because they hadn't been into the senior part of the school before and they were there for the day. We tried to make it as friendly as possible for them, but it had to be very formal. The papers all had to be collected up and put in the envelope and taken to the head. I think he posted them off to the education office. It was all done on the day; certainly no marking or anything like that happened.

The results went to the junior school because they were not actually our pupils. We would see the pupils who hadn't passed after the September when they came to join us. I don't think the children made any fuss about it, they were used to doing exams and they'd been prepared for it and this was the day you did it. Those who passed the 11+ went to school at Sudbury on the bus. Those who didn't stayed at the secondary modern. In some ways, I think it's quite good that those who actually passed went off, because we were a small enough town so that there wasn't the actual sort of rivalry between the schools. In a large town that would have both the grammar and the secondary modern schools, there could be some rivalry. We didn't have any of that because those who went to Sudbury, well they just went and that was that. The rest stayed on with us and that was fine.

Hazel Smith

I remember my first day as a teacher at Cangle because my three children came with me and I put the youngest one in the nursery, took the oldest one to her class and I went out on duty, and the other daughter, when it was time for her to go to her new class, but she'd never been to school before, wouldn't let go of me and she clung to my leg and the teacher who had to take her had to peel her off my leg and carry her away screaming and that was my first day. When I first started at Cangle, Mr Woods was the headmaster and then we had Miss Moore and then Mr Blanchard and Mrs Sparrow, but there have been too many to mention really. I liked it because it's the first place I worked where everyone was really friendly and I'd worked in lots of schools up till then. I'm the last person to have ever taught at the Old Cangle still teaching at the New Cangle.

There was a little courtyard between the buildings with black slate tiles on them and we used to have rabbit hutches there and I used to look after the rabbits and you couldn't hear the traffic from there, and it was always cool and it was just like having a little secret place, the children used to take it in turns to come every lunchtime to feed the rabbits and because it was enclosed with gates, we could let the rabbits out and they could just go in the courtyard.

One of them was called Buster, there was one that used to bite everybody, it was a horrible thing, and there were some really nice ones, there were two black ones, a white and a grey one, I think the grey one was called Ben and the big black one was called Buster.

Susan Dockery

I was acting deputy head at Cangle on two or three different occasions, but never Head and I also went to Cangle as a child.
At Old Cangle I had reception classes and I taught everything up to seven years old. I can tell you about one dreadful PE lesson that I had. It was in the big hall at Old Cangle. I had quite a lot of children and it was an odd shape, it was long and narrow and I tended to stay in the middle, so that I could watch children there and there, but when Cangle was very full of children, that particular hall was used as three classrooms and round the edge it still had wooden slats where the books used to go and they'd never been taken down, and I didn't know, but there were some nails that were protruding from these wooden slats and I had a boy, he was moving round the hall, and he caught his leg on one of these nails and it just gashed his leg open and it was so deep that it didn't actually bleed, you could see all the layers of skin and fat inside his leg and it was horrible, I was so frightened. I see Stephen Fletcher sometimes and he invariably says to me do you remember when I cut my leg, I've still got the scars.
As a teacher we used to have to do dinner duty and when we did a dinner duty one of the perks was we had a free school dinner and we had a cook at Old Cangle, her name was Mrs Coleman and she was a typical cook, you know, she was round and plump and a red face, where she was always baking in the school kitchen, and she used to cook the most beautiful dinners, she really did, and I used to say to her sometimes, Mrs Coleman you try to make me the same shape as you are, and she used to laugh. Lovely pastry, she used to make.
Albert was the best caretaker any school could ever have. He was a wonderful man and his wife Beryl, she used to be an ancillary helper at the school and during the war she was a nurse at the West Suffolk Hospital, so she had good first aid skills, so if anybody ever hurt themselves or was poorly, we always sent for Mrs Wade.
We used to have great fun with the cleaners, because the cleaners were local people, I'm a local person, I grew up in Haverhill, and the cleaners that we used to have, they were also Haverhill people and they used to come in to clean and they'd always have something to tell you about Haverhill. We used to come in and say hello Winnie, what have you got to tell us today and Winnie would always have something to tell you. When I went home at night, my husband would say have you had a good day, what had Winnie got to tell you today? And that was a standing joke.
When I first started teaching, everything was done from the blackboard, it was what teachers used to call chalk and talk. It was all right for some children, but the bright children would be very, very bored because they'd done it all before and the lower children couldn't keep up, When I first came to Cangle, we taught children to read by a special method. It was called ITA and it stood for the Initial Teaching Alphabet and what it consisted of was 34 letters and symbols and each letter or symbol made its own particular sound. With ITA you could sound out, write any word you wanted and you could read it. Absolutely fantastic.

Marion Gregory

The school had changed little, other than in name, from the old Senior School from which it had emerged, and both buildings and equipment were reminiscent of an era closer to my own parents' schooldays than even to my own! The teaching staff were great, with some wonderful characters, led by " Bill" Underwood, one of the most benevolent of men, with his Deputy, Marion Castle, a most capable lady of boundless common-sense, who had taught most of the children's parents and not a few grandparents. This gave her great authority in the town, as in the school, and her every action was taken in the best interests of the children in her care. There was however, little motivation or expectation from anyone in the community for academic achievement by our "11+ Failures" and little in the school accommodation, equipment, or in-service training facilities to motivate the very conscientious teachers, who did their best in the circumstances.
In the teaching of Mathematics I found that the syllabus consisted almost entirely of Arithmetic, still very important in those pre-decimal days of £sd, and where hour after hour of routine slogging through Reduction, Long Division, Long Multiplication of Weights and Measures or Money, made excellent training for a working life at the factory production line, or labouring in the fields, which seemed to be the accepted ambition for the majority of our pupils whatever their ability. I recall seeing one of the lads who left shortly after my arrival, riding a shop bike down the High Street delivering groceries, a bright boy who could easily have gained quite a few O-levels, or done well in an engineering apprenticeship, and resolved to do what I could to change this situation as soon as possible. This was not so easily achieved though, as I was having great difficulty in getting on the same wavelength, and found myself battling with disciplinary problems which I thought I had overcome very early in my career.

The situation in the Science Lab was even worse. Most of the apparatus had gone with the Grammar School, leaving only the most basic of essentials, allowing for very little practical work by the pupils, in very restricted lab conditions. Having been used to labs of standard 40 X 25 feet, I found myself in a room less than one third of that size. Cupboards at the back of the room contained dozens of unlabelled bottles of all sizes, and three benches filled the rest of the room. These were fitted with sinks which leaked all over the floor, and had traditional swan-necked taps, all loose in their sockets which produced fountains to the ceiling whenever the main stopcock was turned on, the kids with considerable foresight having turned their taps on in readiness for such an opportunity.

There was just enough room for me to squeeze between the front bench and the blackboard to do my thing, which was mainly by demonstration rather than practical work by the children, which was all but impossible. The blackboard, being far too small for my expansionist ambitions, led me to acquire an ancient blackboard and easel, the like of which I had never used in my career thus far, but found that there was insufficient room to erect it in the narrow space. Being ever resourceful I found that I could partly open two lower cupboard doors adjacent to my spot, wedge them with a couple of bricks, and balance the board upon them. This was fine until, in a fit of over-enthusiastic board-rubbing, the thing collapsed and guillotined down on my foot, breaking a big toe in the process. Unfortunately, the doctor was not convinced that it was broken, so didn't give me any time off, and I had to carry on working and wearing shoes. I still have a most peculiar toe as a trophy of this episode.

On another occasion, I was giving a lesson on Carbon Dioxide, and had reached its application in Fire Extinguishers. I had gone through the bit explaining how striking the knob would break the glass phial of acid to mix with the carbonate, and grabbed the fire extinguisher from the wall to add a little life to the proceedings. I had not bargained for the fact that some one, at some time in the past, had already depressed the plunger, broken the phial and left it for the next idiot to come along.........! Mayhem ensued, but all was not a total write-off as, with great presence of mind, I availed myself of the opportunity to settle a few old scores before directing the deluge safely into the nearest sink!

One very nice idea, but one which shows how little pressure there was on the curriculum, was Activities Afternoon. This was for the Fourth Year Group, our final year at that time. I had always been fascinated by Photography, and had done quite a bit of developing and printing during my RAF service. I only had a very inexpensive camera as we were very hard-up, and still did my own processing for the sake of economy. I therefore offered this as an option, and had a really smashing group who became interested in it. They were able to bring their own films for D & P, and we were able to use the Lab as a darkroom.
On one of these occasions, one of the lads happened to spot a large inverted image of the view outside the door, projected on to on the end of the bench which faced the door. This was the most stunning Pin-hole Camera effect I have ever seen, the sunny scene 4 outside perfectly reproduced through the door keyhole. We put a sheet of white paper up to enhance the image, and they were amazed that this was in full colour! Of course, at that time all photography and television was in black and white, and even the cinema was mostly so. Suddenly a boy walked past and,Yes! - it was a moving image too. A boy was dispatched outside to give us a show, but was in the middle of his Whirling Dervish demonstration when the Headmaster came by on his tour of inspection! The boy was hauled back into the room by the scruff of the neck, and there followed some embarrassed explanation as to why this sort of behaviour was

being condoned, let alone encouraged. My reputation hung for a moment in the balance, but on being given an Action Replay, Mr Underwood was totally impressed, and my stature rose to new heights. After this I could do no wrong!
In those days, when classes were all "streamed" by ability, it was necessary to create a group of children who did not readily fit into any other category! There were many favourite euphemisms given to label these groups, and I forget which we used, so I shall refer to them as the "Special Class". These children, who have various difficulties with academic work, are generally especially gifted and quick-witted in the Black Art of disruption. Ever watchful for the slightest sign of hesitancy on a teacher's part, or of any momentary lack of continuity in lesson preparation, they would latch upon with the speed of light, and in unison take the opportunity for some sport. Total shambles would ensue!

We were particularly favoured in having some real characters in this group, and one boy who comes to mind was reputed to have a delicate visual problem which made him likely to go blind if he suffered any blow to the head. This was unfortunate as there were daily occasions when the temptation to deliver such unauthorised action was very difficult to contain, the problem being that the part of the anatomy which gives offence is the one which tempts the hand of retribution! Having been warned of this risk I kept my hands firmly in my pockets when dealing with this young gentleman. So, imagine my amazement, on Yard Duty one day, to see two of his cronies, each holding one of his legs, swinging him round in a circle, banging his head each time on a nearby drainpipe! I took a leisurely stroll over to stop them before too much damage was done. We all have our moments.

Percy Kibble was a grand old man, a Haverhillian character who it was a great privilege to have known. He had been, in his working life, a blacksmith, though this was way before my time. His main claim to fame was his music, and he was Organist and Choirmaster at the Congregational Church, which stands more or less opposite to his home. This was on the corner of Priory Road and Hamlet Road, a house more recently occupied by Terry Withers, of Withers" Garage fame, another personality who showed great kindness to me, especially in his efforts to keep my ancient car on the road. In its Victorian Hey-Day the churches in Haverhill seem to have vied to install the most splendid organ, .and even the Town Hall was a contender in this competition. The Congregational Church was leading, and this was Percy's pride and joy. He told the story or a group of the WI who visited the church, and the group became separated as Percy waxed lyrical about his instrument. When they rejoined the party, the lady concerned explained the delay; " My Dear, Mr Kibble has been showing me his Organ! ......It's the biggest in West Suffolk!"

Mr Kibble taught Music in the school, and did so with such enthusiasm and panache that it was thoroughly enjoyed by everyone. As he was not a qualified teacher however, his lessons had to have a member of staff sitting in, so two classes at once were an economic necessity, and we all took our turns at this. As the New Boy my turn was the last period Friday afternoon, and the class? - the Special Class of course! On Day One Mr Kibble gave me my instructions. I was to sit at the teacher's high desk at the front corner, and maintain order without interrupting the flow of the lesson. As his technique was to wind the kids up to fever pitch, this was not an easy assignment. In my previous school I had found that to fix a youngster with a look of authority and hold it, was quite sufficient to remind him of his lowly status in the universe (known in the trade as "Glower Power"), so I tried this ploy. The boy in question treated me an equally steady gaze in return, then hideously crossed his eyes and distorted his face into the most grotesque sight I had seen in years. Fortunately my sense of humour came to my rescue, as I collapsed in laughter, and once again mayhem ensued. Anyway, the lad warmed to me after that, and though I never really got a grip on the group, they never gave me any real trouble from then on.

Percy must have been the last person in Haverhill to drive a pony and trap. His horse was Bess, and he promised me a ride in this outfit. One day during the holidays he came up to Fern Grove where I then lived, and took my four-year old son and me for a ride up Camps Road and into the country lanes. This was the first and only time I have ever had this experience, and remember well the sheer delight of this gentle form of transport. Sitting well above the hedges, the view was so much more interesting, the horse knew where it was going so needed little attention, and all the sounds of the countryside could be heard along with the clip-clopping of the horse's feet. Progress is not all good!

In school, the musical highlight of the week was the Wednesday morning Hymn Practice, and this was enjoyed by everyone within earshot of the school. After we had moved to Eastern Avenue, I heard how the ladies who worked in Eric Radford's Accountant's office next door, missed our enthusiastic renderings. For this event it was necessary to open the screens between rooms, joining three rooms together, and to re-arrange the desks and chairs. After the session, the three classes (about 110 children), and their teachers, had to restore order from chaos, mark the register and get the class away without delay. A new teacher called Bill Childs had been appointed to teach Biology and PE, and had his class in the nearest of these rooms, through which access to the centre room had to be gained. He had sorted his room out, registered, sent off his class through the mob waiting to be let in, and should by then have been settling down to work, when he burst into my Lab next door with a wild look in his

eyes, and proceeded to have what I took to be an instant nervous breakdown. We were just 15 minutes into the work of the day, and he had already had Forty-Six interruptions! The new school could not come a moment too soon!
Teaching Mathematics was not without its adventures, either. The rooms were so small and the classes quite large, around 36, that once in their desks it was not possible to reach individual pupils. This did not well suit my teaching style, which was to do the blackboard bit, then move about the class giving direct help and supervision on a one to one basis. I was occupied at one side of the room and was distracted by something happening at the other side, so went as close as I could to see what was going on. There were a few guilty looks, and one lad was obviously hiding something in his hand. I stretched my hand out - "Give!" He was a big lad, but sat there and looked uncomfortable. I jerked my hand a couple of times, raised my voice a semi-tone - " Come On!". He hesitated again, then a wisp of a smile came across his face, and he dumped into my hand a handful of maggots! They had only been having maggot racing along the pen rack! This young man (of forty years ago!), whose name I can well remember, and with whom I have met and relived this incident on several occasions, was and possibly still is well known in fishing circles in the town, and I hope that he enjoys retelling this story as much as I do.

On another occasion, the first day of a new term, we were in a room adjacent to the reception class of the Primary School, and were quite distracted by the crying and wailing from next door. Several of my girls were overcome with sympathy, and burst into tears too, but they knew that these little ones would spend their next six years in the building, so had every reason to be sympathetic!

A key-stone of the old school was George Hunter, who was reaching the end of his career, but was as quick-witted as ever, with a stock of puns to fit every conversation. He had a reserved chair in the corner of the staffroom, and woe betide any of us who dared to sit in it! He and Marion Castle would do the Daily Mail crossword in ten minutes orally in the lunch-hour. The two of them had a standing joke about me, as I had resorted to scrounging anything I could from anyone I could to supplement the limited resources of the laboratory. I became known as the Magpie, though I did stop short of thieving, if only just. My wife will say that I haven't changed a lot, by the look of my workshop, garage, toolshed, greenhouse, loft, etc., etc........! One day a low-loader with a mechanical excavator pulled into the school site in front of the staffroom window, creating much interest. " Oh. just some thing else for the Science Lab", says George.

Mr Hunter taught Rural Studies, the posh name for Gardening. As he was a chain smoker, I have no doubt that this suited him well, though what he did in the garden we didn't enquire about. It falls to the lot of teachers of this subject to get more than their fair share of the Special Class, and he had a fund of stories about them. My favourite was when they were asked, before an important visit, to rake the cinder path which then ran along the front of the building. One lad was moving forward as he used his rake, so was leaving footprints behind himself. He was not too happy about this, so asked his teacher what to do. "Oh!", says George "you have got a rake that leaves footprints, go and get one that doesn't". Back came the lad with another rake, and by chance started to rake properly. "This one doesn't leave footprints, Sir", says the lad. " Well done", says George!

The term after my arrival, Mr Ken Williams was appointed as Head of Technical Subjects, which included Woodwork, Metalwork, Technical Drawing and allied subjects. We became good friends and were, over the following years, able to develop some innovative courses linking our subject areas, not only catering for the brighter pupils, but providing courses to stimulate and challenge those of all levels of ability.

On one occasion, comparing notes about routine matters, we found that certain lads who were giving me trouble were also trying it on with him, so we evolved a plan. A few days later, I had one of these characters in a Science lesson, and he started playing up. For the time being I continued to set up the apparatus, and was using an ordinary retort stand. " This isn't quite big enough", I said to him, "Go and ask Mr Williams for a long stand". Off he goes, glad for a break and a walk round. "Can I have a long stand for Mr Haigh, please". "Yes, Just wait over there". You can guess the rest. You can imagine his reception when he eventually returned red-faced to the Lab, his pals in the meantime having seen the joke. Much more effective than putting him outside the room.

Mr Williams stayed in Haverhill, and eventually became Deputy Head of Castle Manor Upper School. There was, of course the original Mr Williams, who had joined the school with his evacuated school from Tottenham, early in the war, and was Senior Master at that time. As well as doing all the time-tabling, he ran the Adult Education Centre in the School, so was a key figure and a very wise gentleman. All these people welcomed me warmly, and made what was a difficult time for me, very happy.

There were of course many other teachers who will be remembered for one reason or another. Mr Harvey was one such. A little older than me, he was in charge of Boys' PE, also teaching Maths. He was a fine cricketer, and I am sure that had he not spent

his younger adult years in the more demanding service of His Majesty, he would certainly have played at County level, if not beyond. A man of the most urbane temperament, he was unfailingly polite and well-spoken, in short a real gentleman. I never saw him angry with children or adults, and he exercised authority with a twinkle of good humour and understanding. In those days, before feminism, we invariably allowed the girls to precede the boys, and Mr Harvey would say "GIRLS FIRST", because that was how they wrote it in their Composition books!
He was very fit, and in his forties could outrun even the most athletic of boys. He loved his job, and said to me that teaching sport was for him a lucrative hobby. I took his point, though "lucrative" was not a word that immediately sprang to mind in connection with our pay scales at that time!

On one occasion he had gone up to the school field during the lunch break. This was up Wratting Road, on the right, possibly where the new Upper School is now situated. On the field was a man "exercising" his dog, so Mr Harvey reminded him that this was a school playing field, and that dogs were prohibited for good reasons. The man asked if he knew who he was. The reply came that this was of no consequence. It then appeared that this was the County Advisor for Physical Education, who then received a most polite expression of surprise at his lack of awareness, and that it was very nice to meet him after all these years!
Of course PE is not a subject which one can go on teaching forever, and Mr Harvey eventually left to gain promotion in teaching children with learning difficulties. We all had a soft spot for our "Specials".

Former pupils will also remember Miss Phillips (Domestic Science), who later became Deputy Head in Hungerford; also Mr MacGregor, a brilliant artist, whose work and whose relationship with children I greatly admired. He was still at Castle Manor when I left the town, so may well still be around. Mr Farrar also stayed with the school concentrating on Woodwork. Mrs Hazell taught French, but left before me, and I lost touch.

In June 1958, we had some unexpectedly heavy rain, so much that the Melbourne Brook from Withersfield became swollen, swept down to Haverhill, and broke its banks where it goes into the culvert west of the school before re-emerging along the Pightle. Overnight the whole section of the road from Bradnam's yard to the centre of town was under water, and all the houses and shops were in two or three feet of water. It was a school day, though this was of course cancelled as the building was surrounded by water. On this occasion the water did not actually get inside the building so far as I am aware, although I believe the Headmaster's house was slightly flooded. I used to cycle to school in those days, and had reached the bottom of Crowland Road when I met the water. Quite a crowd of people were there surveying this unusual scene, and were watching one of our lads, on his bike, making circles in and out of the water. He was one of our resident comedians, so was playing to the gallery, and venturing into deeper and deeper water on each circuit. Of course the inevitable happened, the bike came to a standstill in the deepest part, and off he came. He picked himself up, saturated, from the swirling, muddy water, and looked for his bike. This had disappeared from view under the waves, and we were then entertained by his efforts to find it!

Floods in Wratting Road 1968 *History Group*

As it happened, this was pay-day, the day when our Salary Vouchers were sent to school from County Hall. The custom was that these were taken "en-bloc" to the bank by the Senior Master, by whom we would later be paid out. We were terribly hard up at that time, and never had anything left at the end of the month. Moreover there were no such things as Credit Cards, or any facilities for credit available to respectable people, so I was looking at a very bleak week-end. It was therefore a matter of the utmost importance that I got to the school, even if it meant swimming the torrent. Thankfully it did not come to that, as by some ingenuity I found a route around the periphery of the water on my trusty bike, and Bankruptcy was narrowly averted!

There was a further flood, more serious than this one, in September a year or so later, but we had gone by then. The water got into the building that time, and armies of Mums moved in to clean up. As a result of this second inundation, the flood park at Melbourne Bridge was built, which has effectively protected the town ever since.

Our new school was due to be ready in September 1959, but was a few weeks behind schedule. Unfortunately, Mr Underwood had become seriously ill a few months earlier, and our Deputy, Miss Castle, took charge. In the end she had to arrange the whole move, and did it brilliantly. My big worry was in disposing of the legacy of those dozens of bottles of chemicals, which had weighed on my mind for the previous eighteen months. I had tried every possible agency I could think of, and no one wanted to know. In the end, a colleague and I got some lads to dig as deep a hole as possible in a derelict corner of the site, and I spent a dangerous afternoon smashing these bottles into it. Forty years on, I have not heard of any ill consequences of this environmentally unfriendly act, so suppose I am now out of the woods, but have had moments of doubt over the years about this drastic solution!

The move went well, and a new era began. Mr Underwood did return to duty, not wanting to pass up his chance to run his new school, promised for so many years. He retired, however, the following year, and other problems followed, but due to the foresight and efforts of my colleagues and myself, by 1963 we were able to enter students to GCE and other external examinations, and the best of them left the school with five O-levels to take up promising careers.

My future also went well. When the school was due to be reorganised to become Castle Manor Upper School, I elected to transfer to Middle Schools , and in due course became Deputy Head at Castle Hill, from where I later moved to Bedfordshire as Head of a Middle School. After ten fulfiling years there I retired, and now my wife and I live happily in Somerset.

Alan Haigh

Cangle School present day *Printwise*

NURSES MEMORIES

I went back to Cangle later as a nursing auxiliary classroom helper, I think it was called, from about 1965 or '66. I loved every minute of it. Again, I was for years the superintendent of the local St Johns ambulance and I was a nurse during the war, so I had a lot of experience with first aid and nursing. I did all that in the school. I used to have to look after the children. I had to go round and look at their hair. If the secretary was away I used to do the office, all sorts of things. I had quite a bit of responsibility. I used to order all the stock, well tell them what I wanted and I used to have to give the stock out to the teachers and put the orders in to the office. We had over a thousand children there at one time and we had to have classrooms in the west end church because there were over a thousand pupils. I think we had 33 classes if I remember at that particular time. That was when they put prefabs up in the playground and utility buildings, I think they called them. They were big classes, sometimes they had 40 in a class. When I used to give the stock out we used to have to take it over to the west end, unless we were lucky enough to catch the teacher to take it.

I worked through three or four headmasters while I was there. Mr Hutchinson was headmaster. He's the one who gave me the job so he was there when I went there, him and Mr Danes. Then he moved up to when the Chalkstone was built. We had a Mr Wood. We also had a Miss Moore. I got on very well with all of them.

Because I was with the infant teachers I used to help them with all their lessons, it was lovely.

When I was working there they used to have a terrific lot of outings. They used to go on trips, they called it education trips. We used to go to Chadacre Farm and different places all around. We didn't do that as a child, except as a very, very special treat.

In 1977 it was the centenary and we had the school open and we had the most fantastic fête. My husband Albert was working there then as caretaker and I'd been there some time. I used to organise everything, but everything I'd done, I had the backing of him, he helped me. If I wanted a stall set up, he did it and that sort of thing. We had this marvellous day and it was a hot, sunny day, it was wonderful. The playgrounds, the back and the front and the whole school was open. We had all the parents helping and we made a lot of money. We had some mugs made. We had parents serving ice creams, we had all sorts of games and stalls where you made money, fancy dress parades. The children just loved helping, they were all involved.

Once a year the school dentist came and all children were checked by him and he'd make a note and letters were sent home. Sometimes they were done through the school but lots of the parents took them to their own dentist's, but at least it was a

regular thing. We also had a photographer every year and I used to have to round the children up and take them in, make sure their hair looked nice and all the rest of it, and their ties straight. We used to get the families together and the single ones and that was a very popular thing in the school in those days. We used to do that once a year.
We used to have eye tests once a year. Hearing; Dr Gonzales, he used to come and he'd test their hearing. And they'd have their medicals, they were medically examined. I used to have to be in with them because he was a man and that's when it started, they had to have someone there. They were well looked after really, and things were spotted early. It was up to the parents obviously to follow it up, but if there was any deficiency in the sight or the teeth, a letter was sent home.

Beryl Wade

LEAVING SCHOOL

I was very nervous when I left as I was going to Sudbury because if you went to higher education you went out of the town then. I was actually the youngest of that year because my birthday wasn't until the December so I was really only just over 101/2 when I left there. But a lot of my friends went too. We used to have to catch a school bus which went from about three-quarters of the way up the main street every morning to go to Sudbury.

Christine Hart

In some ways I thought it was great to leave school. Once you've left school you realise that it wasn't so bad after all. Rather like when you're in the Army, when you leave you think there were some good times we had then, but at the time you think, well, that's not much of a life, this. Then when you look back your attitude has changed completely. You mellow quite a bit.

Derek Bacon

I didn't want to leave that school. I was quite happy just to stay there, like forever. It wasn't that bad once you actually went up to middle school it was absolutely fine. We had a uniform at middle school, so that was a change to begin with because you're structured in what you wear. And obviously where you may have got a hug from the teachers and what have you at primary school, it's different and the teaching's different and it's a different school. All the teachers knew me throughout the school and you're going somewhere you don't know and obviously some of your friends go to different middle schools as well, so you're not actually going all together and the classes are split. Once I was up there I was absolutely fine, but I did miss Cangle for quite a while.

Jane Duffy

I felt very sad when I left school. I think in those days when you left school it was sad in a way, but I think kids are like that now a lot. I think they still don't like leaving school entirely. I think when we left in those days we were sad because it was something really quite a part of your life, you felt grown up when you left school then.

Gladys Ely

I felt sad when I left. I'd already got a job, I'd written round. My father said write round and get a job, don't wait till you leave and I did and I got a job. But when I left you're leaving all your friends that you've been with, what three years, your teachers who in those days were friends rather than teachers. It was a bit of a sad time. Then you've got to go out into the world and suddenly become adult, which was hard.

Gwen Salmon

Well, I was a bit downhearted when I knew I had to leave school. About a month before I started work, it was getting me down. I kept thinking if I could get back into school somehow, I really loved it. I loved the people who I was scholars with, my companions.

Percy Sizer

All we were thinking about was getting out to work. At that time of day, there wasn't any money about. There was me, my sister, two brothers, mother and father. We were living on one wage, what my father earned. My mother told me to go to work and my father said, if you go to work I'm going to knock off. He said, I want somebody here so there's food on the table for the children when they come home. That's how things were.

Cyril Nunn

No, I wasn't sad to leave the school, I was going somewhere else. I was absolutely delighted. I wasn't leaving the town, and my brother and sister were still there. I didn't feel that I was abandoning the place. I was off to new things.

Jean Pavely

I kept saying I wanted to leave school, but then I think we all cried when we left. On the day we left, all the girls cried. All the boys didn't, and they laughed at us. But we were all crying and we thought it was a terrible thing to have to leave school. All in all, it was a happy time, really.

Hilary Filben

Front of School looking west c1930 *History Group*

I don't think I was sad when I left. It was just a natural progression up to the Middle School. I think I was more apprehensive of the Middle School. You used to get all these stories of having your head shoved down the toilet. Children do that, they tell you all these horrible things. But my sister had started the Cangle by this time and I was quite keen to move on.

Julie Smith

I did miss the school. I didn't want to leave. I do remember getting quite upset when we all left. There was the usual, all the girls cry and the boys don't care. I did really enjoy the school. I can remember a great fondness for it, maybe it's the rose tinted glasses effect. There's a lot of affection for the school. I was very upset when it closed. I would have really liked to have gone back to the school once more and had another look round.

Karen Clark

I wasn't sad to leave to be quite honest. I think partly because I missed so many lessons, I got behind and I was struggling with lessons personally. Mathematics and geography and history; when I went back in they were two jumps ahead of me all the time. I had plenty of friends there and I used to enjoy the sport, but I'd got more going for me on the outside than I had in school.

Tony Stevens

I think there was the fear of going up to the bigger school. Everyone was frightened about that, all the wild stories of what would happen when you get there. I hadn't been at the Cangle long enough to develop any strong attachment to it really.

Gerry Kiernan

We blared our eyes out. What we had at Cangle, there's always something you carry your work around in, it's always a popular thing. At the moment it's rucksacks, isn't it? Well then, it was baskets; you had a basket to carry all your stuff round in. If you were really good, you might have had one of those hideous fabric covers with an elastic bit that went over the top. When you went to Chalkstone, because they had lockers, the baskets wouldn't fit in the lockers so you weren't allowed to take those. That was quite sad.

Jane Farrow

I suppose I regret having to go to a much bigger school and when I was 11, the school I went to was 20 miles away and we used to travel on the bus every day, which is quite a long day out, because we used to leave my house about half past seven in the morning and I didn't get back till nearly five o'clock at night and we had about an hour and a half or two hours homework in the evening as well, so you didn't really finish school until about eight o'clock at night from about half past seven in the morning, so it was a very long day.

Geoffrey Ship

I didn't really enjoy school, I don't think. I don't think many kids did in those days. It wasn't really hard. Looking back, I think we should have enjoyed it, I think we should have made better use of those years. I didn't learn as much as I should have done. It's always the way with hindsight.

Val Gagen

'Best days of your life?' - I would say so. I am probably in the minority, but they were happy days. I can't say I wanted for anything particularly, we had nice friends.

Gwen Salmon

Well, I enjoyed my time at Cangle but I wouldn't say they were the best days of my life.

I was happy enough, yes. I had a brother then and he is three years younger than me and we used to come down together you see. But unfortunately I haven't got him now, he got killed in the war.

Rose Philips

In the class you always got bullies and that. I was the one who was always at the back and very quiet. I always tried to keep out of trouble, but I still got hit for petty things, which I think was very unfair. So I was quite pleased to leave, to be quite honest. School days were definitely not the best days of my life. There were some good times, though. I had many a happy day after school, in the summer holidays and things like that.

Sometimes it was fun at the Cangle. I did enjoy my play and things like that, but I didn't enjoy the teachers. As I got older I thought the teachers were horrible. I thought it was wrong for me to be hit then and I was only a child. Even the teachers at Castle Manor were strict.

Peter Isaacs

It was the best time of my life. I'm glad I was born when I was born. A lot of the local people who I know now say that. We had the best years of our lives.

Percy Sizer

They were happy days, because there were a lot of people who cared, apart from your family. I'm not saying today there aren't people who care, but people are much more self-centred I feel than they were then. They are more materialistic as well, because we had nothing and it didn't bother us. There wasn't the constant demand to get videos and computer games. I mean, life has changed completely now. You can listen to the radio and do other things, whereas the television distracts you somehow. As families we would play cards and do jigsaws which, is obviously a learning process. Family life has changed, because there are lots of things that children can do. In a lot of instances children can only play in their own garden or they perhaps don't live in a road where there is a lot of other children from their school or who are like-minded to them. When I think about the children around where I lived, we all got on and played together.

Diane Basham

They were the most carefree days of my life. You just went off to school in the morning and you came home and everything was there. Your meals were ready, your house was there and you didn't have anything to worry about. They were happy times. And Haverhill was such a lovely place as well, because you knew everyone and everyone was so friendly. There was no traffic and you could just relax and enjoy yourself.

Hilary Filben

They were probably the worst days of my life actually, at school. I never really enjoyed school very much, or even being a kid. I've been much happier as life goes on. It seems to get better really.

Gerry Kiernan

Policeman on point duty c1929 *From a collection of old postcards*

THE CHANGING FACE OF HAVERHILL

In those days the population was 4000 if that. So it was more a community I think than it is now.

When I was a kid here there was no estates round, we literally were Haver in the Hill and Haverhill I think dates back by saying "Haver under the Hill" or some such thing in the olden days.

Withersfield Road: Cobblers shop c1890 From a collection of old postcards

At the back of the Old Corn Exchange there used to be the Haverhill market and the cattle all used to come. It's changed very much I think, I wouldn't like to say what I feel about whether it's for the better or not. There was far more then than there is now. You could go and buy anything in this town, you never used to have to go out to Cambridge. The shop keepers if they hadn't got what you wanted they'd say, "well, right, what is it you'd like" and the next week when they've been to their warehouses you always got what you wanted. I think what is sad now is that we all knew one another in those days and now you don't. Old Haverhill people are gradually dying out and people that came with the over spill are all still here and they had their children and they've grown up and they've got children. Miss Castle knew everyone in those days as a school teacher, she knew their families, she knew their children and she used to say "Oh God I think I'm getting older and I start teaching their grandchildren". It was I think a very happy community in those days and it's sad when that all goes. In those days you only had to come out of your door almost and wherever you went you were going up into the fields and lanes. Miss Castle used to take us all round the fields and we used to pick wild flowers and she used to have little competitions as to who would know the names of most of the flowers. Kids don't have nature studies any longer in that way and I think that's the sad thing.

We all just mucked in all together and after school we used to come home and of an evening as there wasn't much in the town to do. We had two picture palaces then but the girls used to play the boys at rounders on the recreation ground and things like that or take our bikes and go for a bike ride out of the town somewhere. I think it was a strong kind of community and I think it was much more in those days than what it is now. Haverhill as a place has changed considerably, like a lot of places. We used to go out and leave the back door undone and you'd come home and a neighbour up the road would put a cabbage on your water butt or something or a bunch of flowers out the garden, which doesn't happen very much now I don't think. Everybody knew everybody in those days and I think everybody helped everybody. I think they do now but in a different sort of way, there isn't quite the same community feeling I don't think as there was in those days.

I'm sure there must be a lot of the older Haverhill people that would agree that there is nowhere now to go for a nice walk from Haverhill.

You need to go in a car before you can get anywhere to start walking in the countryside and, for me, I don't like it so much. I prefer Haverhill as Haverhill was.

Junction bridge & arches, Sturmer road c1900

From a collection of old postcards

When we were at school there we did value it, I suppose because there was never any rubbish about, you wouldn't be able to put rubbish down. Having said that, my mother would never allow us to go eating a bag of crisps or anything like that. You eat what you eat indoors so there wasn't the rubbish around and the recreation ground was never in a mess, it was always kept well cut by the Haverhill district council as it was then. It was always nice and people used to sit round under the trees and it was somewhere nice to go, but like everywhere else times change, don't they?

There were standards then and they are not kept now. I mean you can go down the street now and people just drop cigarettes boxes and things like that everywhere now. Violence was never a problem in this town anyway. OK, there might have been a fight between a kid at school when it didn't suit you, but no violence like it is now, certainly not. I don't ever recall it. Even with the Forces here, the Army and the Air Force being up the road, no, I don't remember real violence.

Gladys Ely

There was much more freedom in those days. It was a much smaller town, there were only about 5000 people in the town. I'm not saying we knew everybody because of course you don't, but you could go about a lot more than you can now. We played on the railway line, well not actually on the railway line but the railway came through the town. There was a branch line that went to Sudbury which was the Colne Valley line and that actually ran along where the sports centre is, along the road there and out towards Sturmer Arches which is still there, the old railway bridge. Also, we used to play up on Chalkstone Hills which has now got houses all over it. There was a chalk pit up there and we used to go and play there quite a lot. We'd got out first thing in the morning and we wouldn't come home until teatime. Our parents didn't know where we were, but it never occurred to any of us that there was anything to worry about, because there wasn't really. Obviously there wasn't as much traffic as there is now, there weren't as many people about. I never heard of anything happening to any child, no child was ever kidnapped or abused that I ever knew about. That probably isn't to say that it didn't happen, it's just I didn't know about it. It was a very small town and I think people looked after other people's children more. You'd go round to your friends' houses, well that's the way it seemed. But certainly it was much more free from that point of view. Certainly now, children are not as free as they were then. Because, although there's so much more money and they've got so many things, you can't let them out of your sight. They don't have the freedom to grow up and be themselves the way we did because we could just go off and do what we wanted to do. We'd go to Saturday morning pictures and in the afternoon we'd play what we'd seen. We'd go off somewhere and be Tarzan up trees etc. and they just can't do that anymore, it's a shame.

St. Marys Church *Alan Haigh*

It's changed very much. It's so much more impersonal. It's not a particularly violent or crime-ridden town. The statistics prove that it's actually quite a quiet place. But I think there's more fear about than there used to be. You think things might happen and so you are more protective of your children than you were. The centre of the town has changed a lot and for the worse, because there used to be a lot of really nice, old buildings in it. There were a lot of medieval buildings, especially buildings from the late 17th century. There were two or three really nice Georgian town houses. During the '60's virtually the entire street was gutted and rebuilt in '60's style. There isn't anything hardly left of the old Haverhill anymore. You walk down the street now and you could be absolutely anywhere because it's just all the multiples that you see in every other town. There's very little that you can recognise from when you were a child. Sometimes we talk about it and we say, "Where did that sweet shop used to be?" and "Where was the greengrocer's?" and we try and pinpoint exactly where they were. Where the coffee bar was that we used to go to when we were teenagers. All of those things have gone.

When I was about 14 or 15 years old, there were two or three youth clubs in the town and because there were so few of us, we all used to go to one or another of them. Then there was a dance every Saturday night, either in the town hall or in the Bigmore Hall. That's going to be changed now, they're going to open a night club up there, so there will be more things going on. There isn't really anything like that anymore. There's the youth centre, but it doesn't seem to be the same. I think it's because society has changed and the sort of children who want to go to youth centres are not the majority any more, which they used to be.

Everywhere you go now you see signs "No ball games". What do they want the children to do? If they stay indoors all the time and play on their computers, they say, "Kids today, they never do anything, all they do is sit in front of the television". And as soon as they go outside and they want to play, people are complaining about it saying, "They're making all that noise, make them go and play somewhere else". Children have got to play outside their houses because, as I said, you can't let them out of your sight. What is all that grass out there for, if it's not for them to play on?

We used to play in the river too, because the tributary of the river Stour that runs through the town where it goes along where the bypass is now, the relief road that goes past the sports centre. That was water meadows then, there was no road there. There was the railway line and then it was the hills, Chalkstone Hills, where we played. We used to play down on that river quite a lot because all of the houses in the high street on that side, their gardens all ran down to the river. We were also friends with the boy whose father had the jeweller's which was half way up the high street, which is actually still there and he runs it himself now. We used to play there in their garden that went down to the river, so we would play in the river because it was never very deep.

It was a really rural town. It was more like a village than a town really. Well none of this was here, none of these houses were here at all, not even when I first started going to the grammar school. At the top of this road then there was fields and there was an isolation hospital. So when people had scarlet fever or something like that, it was just a bit further up from where we are now. The industrial estate that's down there, none of that was there. When I first moved up Duddery Hill to live in that house where my parents live still now, across from us was a really nice house. It was an old Georgian house with a big garden, which was where one of the doctors lived. Behind that was just fields. It was very different. You have to get a long way up above the town now to be able to see countryside.

Christine Hart

Recreation ground & Banstand *From a collection of old postcards*

You have to remember that Haverhill was then full of servicemen. Up until about '42 there was the Army there and then of course Americans, they were at Ridgewell and other sites fairly nearby, so there was a great intake of servicemen. It livened the whole place up possibly but it was much different.

It was rural then, very much so. You just had the trades people. There was a big difference between trades people and the labour and working class and the middle class as well. Now you can hardly tell that sort of thing but you certainly could then.

Derek Bacon

In those days, as a child, before the war, there was under 4000 here. You knew everybody, you literally knew everyone. You could go up the street, it didn't matter what you wanted, you could get. The shops weren't quite so peculiar to one item, there were shops up there that sold everything. There was a shop at the top of the street, they sold everything from paraffin to furniture. Of course people didn't go out of town to shop in those days. We hadn't got cars and if you went to Cambridge by bus or train, it was quite an excursion, it was a treat. I think there was more to do, I always seemed to have lots to do. There wasn't a sports centre of any sort, we had the recreation ground. But when I was a child, we used to play in the streets. We'd have spinning tops and marbles from one side of the road to the other, things that you couldn't possibly do now.

There used to be an excursion to Cambridge on a Saturday. It was 9d and that was quite a treat. We used to get on the train and go to the seaside, mostly Clacton. The bus went to London in the mornings but such as us didn't go on it very often. Hardly any cars about.

Nowadays, I'm afraid we're one of the those who do ride about in a car. You do need it when you live here I think. It's so different. I was born in this house nearly 75 years ago and I can go up the street now and perhaps don't see anyone I know at all, and I am a person, as I said, I was superintendent of the St Johns Ambulance for years so I did get around and know people. I go to lots of whist drives, I go to bridge drives, we go to different things, we do go out and about.

It's got its good and its bad points. I think the worst thing that's ever happened to

Haverhill as the fact that they took the railway away and made it into an industrial town. Perhaps I shouldn't go onto politics, but to make it into an industrial town and take the railway away, it's the beginning of putting everything on the road, wasn't it? We've got an enormous industrial estate now. Before the war, all we ever had was Mr Gurteen's factory and the laundry, nothing else.

The thing I'm against is the fact that they took the railway away. There were two railways in Haverhill, the Colne Valley that supplied the coal yard and the one opposite the Cangle which was the passenger one. I think that's the biggest mistake that's happened in Haverhill.

We had two cinemas; we had the Playhouse and the Empire. We haven't got either now apart from the town hall who do a bit of films. And they used to come round with the horse and carts with all the deliveries. But now, we've even had to stop having our milk delivered because it was taken; by the time we'd got up in the morning it had gone and we couldn't afford to keep paying for milk we didn't get. This has done away with the country life really, it is now an industrial town.

Beryl Wade

We as youngsters made our own amusement. We would go to the swimming bath or we'd go to the cinema and round our friend's house, or just go for a walk, meet up on the rec and have a laugh and a joke. They seem to want to be entertained rather than find entertainment today, but that's the way the life is, it's not the people's fault I don't think, it's the world has changed. There's the sports centre, there's an arts centre but there doesn't seem to be anything in between. And it all costs money, and money's hard even now, it's tight on lots of families. I have always lived here, since 1940 and I've always liked it, even when the over-spill came down, they used to say they didn't like it, I used to think to myself, well I do. I mean, you didn't argue the toss but the evacuees, I think some of them went back because they didn't like it. It was the quiet, because after having the hustle and bustle of town life it would seem quiet. There's more hustle and bustle here now than there was in those days. You could walk across and wouldn't see a car apart from an Army vehicle. You didn't have cars, you had bikes when I was young. If anyone had a car,

Rose & Crown Public House pre 1906 From a collection of old postcards

they were really well off. Even the bread was delivered by horse and cart, and the milk and the refuse collection.

Fear didn't come into walking around come to think of it. We never feared, we used to go off in the morning and never thought about coming home until late afternoon. You could roam around in those days freer than today and safer I would say. Because being a small area you knew most people most anyway who came across. Years back, just after I started work here, which was 1947, there was only 4,000 population, which meant you knew everybody and I went to school with most of them anyway and knew their parents, their uncles, aunts. You knew the roads and you just knew everybody, so whoever you met out you could say hello to, which isn't so today.

We used to go to the pictures at night and walk home, go to the dances at night, walk home and never thought that somebody was going to accost you, didn't cross your mind. So there couldn't have been that much fear in those days. Today you wouldn't let them cross the road or even let them play in the front garden. Nowadays it's bad. Perhaps you worry too much, but once you hear of one thing you are on your guard. So I would say that we had a safer childhood, a happier childhood in lots of ways. We had a lot more freedom because children today are not free, it's always "don't go there, you mustn't go there, be careful when you go there, don't go there alone". We never had that you see.

Gwen Salmon

The town has changed because obviously it's pedestrianised and all sorts. It didn't seem as big, but whether it's just because you basically only go where your parents take you at that age, you don't wander about. It's developed a lot since then. Cangle seemed to be the centre of it, it was at the beginning of Queen Street and High Street. There was always children in the playground or things happening there. There were open days and fêtes there, there always used to be lots of people about. I've lived here all my life and I quite like it, but it is expanding quite a lot. I do probably feel now that we need more things to keep people here as in shop-wise. The high street was fine then, but it needs to accommodate the larger estates and developments that are going up now.

Jane Duffy

Queen Street from Market Square c1900 From a collection of old postcards

Haverhill has changed in the sense that it's got bigger. People either come and stay, like I've done, or they come and think it's an awful dump and clear off! OK, we had the railway then and you could get into Cambridge on the train, but there was the bus as well. You still needed to go out of town for certain things and I think you still need to go out of town for some of the same things. Things move faster and all that sort of thing but apart from that I don't it's that different. It's still a small place, on the edge of everything, and still complaining about being on the edge of everything. We're neither Suffolk nor Cambridgeshire nor Essex, are we? We're in that odd corner. There's more unemployment, but that's getting better now. We went through a very bad patch. I can remember there were dances at the town hall in the evenings and the village lads would scrap with the town lads over some girl, or somebody would get drunk and throw things. OK, there's more of it now because there are more people. But I actually think, proportionately, it's not that different. You still hear the same sort of things happening. And there are still the same characters who are often in trouble. We had our characters then who were much the same. There are families that go through the school, large families with cousins and so on; a name that goes right through, there's one in each year. It still happens, and it happened then. I don't think society changes that much really. There's progress; more people have cars and so on.

Hazel Smith

We never had any television. When we had our summer holidays we used to try and get into the harvest field and drive the horses away. We'd start off in the morning with a quart of cold tea and a doorstep, we used to call it, with dripping or jam or cheese. We'd go to the farm and see if we could get a job at the farm. We used to get about 3d and then we used to go to the old Empire pictures.

Old Railway Station 1907 *From a collection of old postcards*

We had a good time. We had a crystal set and we used to put it so you could sit down on a Sunday evening and hear the service. We made our own enjoyment. We used to play about in the fields. We used to catch rabbits and sell them for two-pence. It was four-pence if you skinned it. They were bad times really. The wages were poor, about 28s a week for the farm wages. It was hard, but we enjoyed it. I was a tall lad when I was young so I was able to help my mother.

Ted Basham

Everything was delivered so mums didn't have to go out of the house a lot, but there again it took longer to do the household chores. I don't think mums did a lot in the afternoons. They used to change from their working clothes in the afternoon into a dress.

Diane Basham

High Street c1890 *From a collection of old postcards*

We used to make our own enjoyment. On our way to school we played marbles in the gutter. Then we played cigarette cards, pitching the cards up near a wall. Cigarettes then had playing cards in. We used to have tops and also we had the brook going along at the bottom of the recreation ground where we used to have races floating empty tins; cherry blossom tins, OXO tins. We used to have a race and we used to follow it right down the brook to the Black Horse pub. We lost sight of them then. When the council used to mow the grass in the summer we used to build houses on there for a week, grass houses. And we used to have fights on there. We used to make some of the grass into boomerangs, as they called them. We were never miserable, we made our own enjoyments, we loved it. We were never bored. In the summertime, there were the swings on the rec. and our mothers used to make us sandwiches when we came out of school in the afternoons. We used to have empty sauce bottles and our mothers used to fill them up with tea. So we took our tea over on the rec. and had it. We never got bored.

There were fields up Clements Lane where the Clements is now and we used to go and play up there. There were three big meadows up there we used to play in. We had the maypole and we used to get an orange piece of rope. That was lovely going round on the maypole. We used to sit in like a seat and go round. It was a big wooden, tall pole with all these ropes hanging down and then you tied your rope into a loop. You could hang onto it and go round, but we used to like to sit on a rope seat that we made and then go round. You used to start yourself off by running and then sit on the seat. We never had any pocket money much. I only had two whole pennies a week to spend, but we were happy with that. We used to go round people's dustbins collecting jam jars. We used to wash them up and take them down the Co-op and you'd get a halfpenny for a pound jar and a penny for a two-pound jar. We were quite inventive.

I wouldn't want to be a child now. I think we had the best years in this period. We never had much, but what we had we were thankful for. The town itself was friendly. It wasn't like it is now.

Everyone had a garden then, we used to grow all our own vegetables. We had chickens and things. There was a lot of horses about this place then. We used to have to get up in the morning, early before we went to school, and gather some of the manure, what they did on the roads, for the gardens.

Saturdays in our family, one had to clean the shoes ready for Sunday, another one did the knives and forks on a board with bath brick. Another one would help your mother go shopping. One of us would have to go down to the wood yard and get logs. Another one had to go to the gasworks and get coke. So we all had our little jobs. The girls on the recreation ground used to make daisy chains. We used to make our own kites. We used to go up into the fields and cut the bramble out of the hedge and bend it to the right shape. Then we used to get brown paper and a piece of wood about an inch or 11/2 inches wide. Well, you had that for the main stem and then you tied on the bramble. Then we put the brown paper on with flour paste. Then we used to make a long tail with string and newspaper tied on it. We got a ball of string and we used to fly them. There were a lot of us on the green over there flying their kites, see who could get them to go the highest. There was always plenty to do.

One thing, the swings were taken down on a Saturday night over the rec. and put up again Monday morning. You weren't allowed to go and play balls on there on a Sunday. My parents wouldn't let us have a ball out on a Sunday at all. If we did, my father used to take it and put it in the dustbin and that was that. No, Sunday was Sunday. We all went to Sunday School, to different places. I loved Sunday School, it was only for an hour in the morning and an hour in the afternoon, but that was lovely. There were no shops open on a Sunday. Sunday nights our parents used to take us a walk round the fields. We used to enjoy it. I used to wear shorts and jersey. I never had a suit till I left school.

We used to walk everywhere in the old days. It did us good, it was a healthy life. We used to go a lot in the summertime up to Ladygates Woods, although I didn't talk posh like that. We used to call it "Liddygits". It's like a lot of the places round here. We would talk as we were taught. They call that the "Coupals"; well if anybody asked me down the town, where is the "Coupals" I'd say I'd never heard of it. I've heard of the "Couples" because I always call it the "Coupals". That's like "Sturmer". It's "Stirmere" really because there's a mere there, but I'll say "Stumer". Then there was "Barny Distant", well we called that "Banson". And Kedington was called "Kitten", it's still called Kitten. If we were speaking to any of the local people and we said that's Kedington, they'd say we had a dishcloth in our mouth. The Londoners couldn't understand us when they came down here first, the things we had or how we spoke. That's like the garden snails, you call them snails, don't you? Well, we don't, even today we don't. We call them "hoddydods". Then there's the see-saw, this was called the "timpanytauter". I have heard that name on the radio. We never said "girls", we used to say "old maws". If a girl was hurrying up the street, we wouldn't say hurrying. Even today we'd say, "look at the old maw clawing up the street". That's our way of talking. We still use that.

Children are all fighting and vandalising now. It's so different. We haven't progressed at all. They've brought all these people here and these factories, but people still have to go out the town to work. We didn't years ago. It was either the land, or Gurteen's or girls used to go into service.

In my teenage days, there used to be a late train to Cambridge because they ran pretty often. On a Saturday there was a train that went from here at two o'clock, an excursion train that left Cambridge again at half past eleven. That was only 9d. In the summer months when the sea sides were open, you could go from here on a Saturday to Southend. We left here at eleven in the morning and left Southend at half past eleven at night. That was 21/2d. You could go to London on the Pullman. A man came here and started up a bus company and he ran the grey Pullman and you could go to London for 21/2d every day. Life never got dull. I think Haverhill is hell now. It broke a lot of our hearts when we had all this over-spill and how they've knocked the town about. They've pulled down lovely buildings in the town which shouldn't have been pulled down. They haven't done that in Bury

We had more shops than what we've got now. We've got no shops here now. If you want to buy a kettle or any utensils you've got to go to Bury or Cambridge to get it. We've got no ironmonger's here now. We had the Co-op where Peacocks and all lot was, where they sold everything. They sold the corn for your cattle, they had the butcher's, they did their own bread and cake making there. There was all the groceries. There was the furniture part there, the millinery part, the men's outfitters, the furnishings, all under one roof. When we came under Cambridge they done away with it. Life was easier then.

Then we had International opposite there before you got to the church on the other side. Then there was Jarvis's up the street, that was a grocery. Then a bit further up was another grocery, Mr Beare's. Then in Queen Street there was Mr Wilsher's, they had a big grocery. Then there was a lot of these little corner shops. We had four wet fish shops, we haven't got one in the town now. I'm supposed to have wet fish three times a week, but I can't because there isn't any. The doctor's told me not to buy it from the supermarkets because you don't know whether that's fresh or not. They have it on the market on Fridays and Saturdays but, as he said, they've been carting it about since Tuesday. We had fried fish shops all in the town, but they're all scattered now. If I want fish and chips I've got to go onto the Clements from here, or I've got to go over to the Chalkstone. They're cold by the time you get home. The shops on Saturdays were open till nine o'clock, all the little shops. The town was packed with people. Most of the ladies went to work. They did the housework and the washing Saturday afternoons and then they used to go out shopping Saturday nights. In the town there were over 20 pubs.

There were quite a lot of drunk people then, but they never made any scenes. You never heard of anyone getting arrested. People used to go out and have a drink, but they came home quiet. Pubs closed at ten then, there was no noise. The lights used to go out at ten in the street. You wouldn't hear a commotion like you get now, and the fights and that. You knew who they were, the people who used to get drunk but they never interfered with anybody.

I only went in the pub about once or twice. I said no, this isn't my life. I was like a bird in a cage, I used to go in with my pals. They used to drink but I was nobody for drink, never have been. I was sitting there like a bird, waiting to out through those doors to fly out.

Percy Sizer

Queen Street c1920 *From a collection of old postcards*

Haverhill has changed terrific. This council here now, they've done away with all the country walks there were about here. Every Sunday night people would go for a walk round the fields in the summertime. But now they've all gone. This council has just done away with them. All along here by the industrial estate, you could walk along by this hedge and go right the way across there, right across the Bumpstead Road to Sturmer Hall and right the way around, down Potem Hill and all the way around. Wilfsey Meadows, up the Chalkstone Hill there, come out at the top of the Rising Sun. You'd run into different people there and have a chat and that. Some used to stop into the pub, some in the Rising Sun or the Sturmer Red Lion and have a drink and then walk round again. Every Sunday night. We never got bored.

We used to walk from here to Cambridge on the Good Friday, and then walk back. We were all used to walking. We had a tennis ball so we used to half run sometimes. It used to take about 5 hours to get to Cambridge. We couldn't afford to go on the train. When I started to work I was getting twopence farthing an hour. I had 8s 4d a week, that's all for 48 hours.

In the wintertime, down near where the police station is now, there used to be a council yard down there, when the bosses and all of them used to go out for the weekend shooting, they used to take all the rabbits and hares and that down the council yard and they used to make a great big pot of stew. You could go there and buy a bottle of soup and a bit of dry bread down there for a penny.

Harold Sozer

Haverhill was a small country town, it had a market every Friday, a cattle market at the back of the Rose & Crown. They used to drive the pigs and that up there through the streets. When I started work on the farm, I used to bring two horses, down Camps Road, up the High Street. Halfway up there was the smithy. I used to go in there with two horses to be shod.

There were very few cars about. The milk float was pulled by horse and cart. The dustcart was the one with dustbins with a horse. They were most all horses then. We used to get two dustbins and put them in the road and play cricket. There weren't any cars about, well there were cars about but normal people hadn't got cars. We were safe as houses. The only thing we were going to get knocked over by was a horse and cart. When we had a punch, one probably had a nosebleed, one had a black eye and then they all went in and bought each other a pint. There wasn't any trouble.

They use knives and that today, don't they? It's so much more violent. In my books, everything has gone wrong.

I used to be a poacher. I used to love being round the fields. I can't now because I've got arthritis in my knees. Now there are houses covering all the fields. It makes me sad, really. But I can't get out much now anyway, so it doesn't really make a lot of difference, I suppose.

There used to be a railway here. There's no railway there. We've progressed backwards.

I never earned much when I first started work. I believe it was about one pound ten shillings a week for 48 hours. That was on the farm. It was all hard work at that time of day, there weren't any machines. It was all hump and lug. You just had to do it. I loved the farm work. But after a time the wages got so far behind you had to move somewhere else, where there was more money.

Cyril Nunn

Haverhill didn't start to expand until 1959 when they wanted houses for the over-spill from London, and that was the beginning of the expansion. The relief road that goes through Haverhill towards Sturmer was mostly dirt track after Swan Lane. There was a big junkyard off this dirt track, and this man used to take rabbit skins. My father used to be given wild rabbits and I used to take the rabbit skin to this older man and he would give me three pence.

I can't remember any fights in the playground because you were always doing something, you didn't just stand around like youngsters do today. We made our own entertainment, and when we were out of school, we played schools. Our next door neighbour had six or seven children and we used to play shops and doctors and nurses, all the things that were relevant to adult life basically. I remember going on nature walks during school time. But after school as children we had much more freedom, and we could wander through the cornfields, where there were footpaths. There was Bluebell Woods that we used to walk to. On the embankment, where the arches are on the road from Haverhill to Colchester, that was the Colne Valley Railway. We were able to walk across the fields from the back of our house and go up onto the bank of the railway, and we would spend half a day up there and pick things like violets. There were only 4 trains per day on that particular line, so we were quite safe. In the summer you'd see grass snakes, but I didn't like that.

Queen Street 1913 *History Group*

The traffic today I feel is the hindrance to everything because it's fast and children can't safely go across the road. We were very naive and innocent, we were allowed to be children while nowadays they grow up so quickly.

Diane Basham

When we were children, we didn't have anything to play with, but every day used to be full. We used to meet around nine o'clock in the morning and in the summer holidays we had a picnic. We'd either walk up to the old railway line or we'd get our bikes and we'd bike to Kedington or Clare. We'd have a picnic and then we'd get back about teatime. We had such fun and we didn't have to have things to do.

We used to make up our own fun. We used to play rounders, we used to make daisy chains, we used to look for four leaf clovers, all sorts of things. The days seemed to be so long. You could go off on your bike and your mothers wouldn't worry about you because they knew there was no traffic. People seemed so honest. There was very little crime or anything like that, so you were quite safe. The summer holidays seemed so long then, and it always seemed to be so hot every day, lovely long summer days. One of the things we used to do, my friends and I, to while away the days, we used to have a little bottle with a screw cap on and we used to have some cream of the milk. We used to sit and shake and shake and shake this until turned to butter. Then we used to get it out the bottle and put a little salt with it and mash it up and that used to be our butter for the week. That used to keep us amused for some time.

For a treat we used to have a stick of rhubarb and dip it in sugar. Sweets were still on ration then. I think children got a lot more out of life than they do now. We didn't always have what we wanted. My brother used to get into awful trouble because he kept wanting threepence and he wouldn't go to school until he'd had threepence. He stood there kicking the garden fence, but he didn't get it because we didn't have it. We did want things that we couldn't have, but we didn't keep on wanting. If we realised that we couldn't have it then we'd just go off and do something else. It didn't cost much to keep you amused, not in those days really. We could have a whole day's entertainment and it didn't cost you anything.

We didn't go home until it was dark, about nine or half past nine. Our parents weren't worried about us. There were so many places to go in Haverhill, so many places to explore. There were the fields and up the castle. We used to go and make dens up the castle. There were some old ruins up there and a moat and a pond. We used to catch tadpoles and put them in jars and watch them turn into frogs.

I think the most important thing that we had was a bike. We used to be off all day. We used to bike all over the place, to all the villages.

My sister's got four little ones and Craig seems to want to be in front of his computer all the time even on the most beautiful days. Hannah likes to put her make-up on and her nail varnish, do her hair and put her Spice Girls record on and dance to it. They've all got bikes but they wouldn't be safe to go off on them, not like we used to do.

Hilary Filben

I moved from London, so I was used to not being allowed out and you couldn't go anywhere without your mother or your father. Coming to Haverhill, where I could go out and play, I thought it was wonderful. It was a lot quieter than it is now. There were fields by our house, where there are all houses everywhere now. I seem to think it was probably more friendly than it is now. We used to have this wheelbarrow race in the summer. Throughout the High Street there'd be little teams and stopping off at pubs. There were all families and people dressed up and they would stop at the pubs along the High Street and finish at the recreation ground. I found people quite friendly, but I know my parents didn't. They were Londoners and everyone else was yokels and there was definitely this friction between the two. My father didn't particularly miss London, but I know my mother did, especially the shops. Soon after, my grandparents sold their house and moved down here as well. We used to live in a really big house with great grandparents, grandparents, that type of really big London house. My mum actually having her own house, I know she enjoyed that, and actually having a bathroom, because we'd had one bathroom for the whole house. It was a complete change for her.

Julie Smith

When I was about nine or ten, they started building all the new housing estates round the Chimswell and all that type of thing. It was great fun because we were out on the building sites all the time playing. My mum would have probably gone up the wall if she'd have found out what we were up to.

If it wasn't for the fact that my family were there, I wouldn't go to Haverhill because I don't particularly like the place. It's very big now. They build and build and build but they don't build facilities. There's yet another housing estate going up but where are the facilities to cater for the people? If you don't drink, there's not much. They are getting better because you've got the town hall, which has got a lot of stuff in there now, and the cinema and everything, but they need more entertainment stuff. It's always been a problem in Haverhill. When I was young there was never anything to do which is probably why we hung around building sites, of all places. I would never move back, I was quite happy to move out.

Karen Clark

Haverhill was a very nice little town then. You knew every shop owner and you knew most of the people that walked up and down in the street. You could leave your bicycle anywhere, or your motorbike. You could leave your clothes over the seat, go to the pictures and they'd still be there when you came back. You never got anything stolen. In those days, there were two cinemas, which you had to actually queue up or book your seats to get in. We used to go twice a week, Tuesdays and Saturdays. You used to take your girlfriend, whoever she was from class.

There were two dance halls, the town hall and another one over the top of the Co-op which was called the Bigmore Hall. It's just now going to be re-opened as a night-club.

The Rose and Crown was the real classiest hotel of the lot then. I always remember one friend of mine who was a bit of a rebel. He said he wasn't going to eat any of that old school dinner rubbish, he was going to go over the Rose and Crown and have a proper dinner over there.

It all started to change in the late '50's when it was one of the first London over-spill towns. They started building factories and they brought all these Londoners and they built these new estates. Regrettably, they brought all the habits that Londoners bring with them, like litter and thieving. The whole town is a bit like a ghost town at nights now. The period of time when I was at school, there were a lot of airforce and military people based all round about. The whole town used to be buzzing with people. You could hardly walk on the pavements on a Saturday night because there were so many people there. They used to have the big Haverhill "Gala", where they had all the floats. They used to have these beauty competitions and some of the girls used to get on the carnival float. It was a nice little town in those days.

Everybody respected the policemen. If a policeman saw a group of boys misbehaving themselves, or potentially misbehaving themselves, he'd come up there and he'd either just wave his gloves at them and tell them to go away. If he actually caught them, he would just give the culprit or the ringleader a clip of the ear. That was all the respect they needed in the town, because they were walking around, you never knew where they were going to be.

Tony Stevens

Parade c1920 *From a collection of old postcards*

The town centre has changed a lot. The right-hand side remains much the same, but the building on the left was the old International Stores, now long gone. Beyond this is the old butcher's shop. This was a timbered building, very old, and I wonder if it was possibly the only one to survive the great fire of 1665. The windows, open in summer, were covered with fly screens, and the butcher, whose name escapes me, but who was hugely cross-eyed, stood behind the half closed stable-type door at his circular block, hurling his cleaver at a joint of meat, and I always marvelled at his skill at having kept his full complement of fingers! The position of the corner of this building was exactly where the white line of Camps Road, if projected, would meet the centre of the High Street. Driving out of Camps Road was like Russian Roulette, and the trick was to use the Co-op window to see the closest on-coming traffic, then gingerly edge out for a longer view! The houses of Peas Hill have now long gone.

Alan Haigh

When we lived in London there used to be huge parks all around us and there was quite a bit of freedom of there. Then arriving in Haverhill, in the middle of the countryside, we expected to have a lot of freedom and not necessarily having much freedom at all because you couldn't go into the countryside because it all had crops. One of the differences for me was that in London we lived in the Irish catholic community. Most of the kids I knew then, my parents would have known their parents, or known of them. There was more of a community feel, even though it was probably spread out over an area. And it wasn't just a locality community, it was a type of Irish catholic community.

That changed quite a bit when we moved to Haverhill. There are quite a few Irish Catholics in Haverhill but that was diluted quite a bit. One of the things I was more aware of was that my parents didn't know what was going on as much as they would have done before. There was that bit of extra freedom almost. They didn't know what was happening with me because it wouldn't always be reported back, whereas otherwise it would be. They'd use to know who I was with and what we were doing. Haverhill has changed enormously. When I arrived we lived on the Clements. The Chalkstone was just being built. The Parkway was obviously well established by then. The Clements still had a lot of empty houses on there. I would have thought the population then couldn't have been much more than five to seven thousand, probably nearer five even. Now it's more like 20,000, so it's miles bigger than it was then. Then it was almost totally dominated by council estates. Most of the newer housing today is private housing and some housing association places as well, so there is more of a balance.

Gerry Kiernan

High Street 1958 — *Alan Haigh*

THE CANGLE FOYER

It's something completely different from what we've been used to. It's helping young people which is what the idea is and I think that's a good idea if it doesn't become a sort of drop-out centre rather than educational. I think there is going to be quite a lot of staff there and different people coming and giving training to the youngsters, which is a good idea helping them to get jobs and filling in their CVs and so on.
I think that is a good idea providing it doesn't deteriorate over a very short time. Because as much as the staff try you can't stop people turning these place into rubbish tips at times.
It will be nice to see the old Cangle used if it's going to used for people who will actually learn from it. The ideas are absolutely super if it does work. I'm sure the people will want to make it work, but it can only work if the youngsters themselves will participate and learn from it and value it.
I would be very interested in going down when it opens to see what's going on. Unfortunately I'm too old to do anything that way now, but I would have loved, I think, to have gone and helped in some way. Not worked, but serve teas or something in the voluntary capacity.
I probably would go and have a meal once a week or something like that which it would be nice to think older people might go down there and use it as a community sort of centre. But sometimes the old and the young don't mix so easily.
I think it would be nice to think it was a non smoking place, but if you do it as non smoking, are you then not going to get many youngsters go? Because it is for youngsters that smoke these days, isn't it?

Gladys Ely

I'm glad something's being done with it because I was afraid they were going to knock it down, they were talking about doing that at one time just so they could improve the road, which I thought was an absolute scandal because there are so few buildings left of any worth in the town. Apart from the parish church, virtually the only things that are left in the town are the Victorian buildings and that is one of the major ones in the town. I'm really glad it's being used for something. It would have been a pity if it had just turned over to ordinary housing because then it would probably be quite expensive because it's such a beautiful building. It's nice that there will still be access to it.
I think that it's nice for people, especially young people, to learn about what the building was like before it's like it is now. Obviously as time goes by there are going to be fewer and fewer of us left in the town who actually went to that school as it was. It will be very good for future generations to be able to read about what it was like to go to school then and how very different it was from what school is now.

I think the way that the Cangle School is being renovated is very sympathetic which is good because it could have been altered beyond recognition and just the shell of it kept. But it hasn't been and I think that's really nice. It's such a landmark in the town and people who've lived here all their lives, it's one of the main things that you look for.

Christine Hart

I really don't understand in some ways. OK, I'm old, blinkers on you could say, I'd far rather have seen the school brought up and used as a school as originally planned. With money spent on it, it could have been modernised no doubt. On the other hand, it's serving a very good need. I wouldn't have any firm views against it. To see the place dressed up is nice anyway. Some rather clever work has gone on there. I like that Victorian type building anyway, it's really nice. I'm pleased it's being used for something. It would be terrible to just pull the whole lot down, I'd have been really annoyed about that.

Derek Bacon

Being in the building trade, I've watched what's been done and I believe they're doing a very good job there of preserving as a building, keeping it mostly as it was. I only hope the outcome will be fully successful with what it's going to be used for. I believe the people were a bit concerned who live near, but I just hope their fears won't be necessary.

Albert Wade

It was a very happy school life at my primary school. When I walk past Cangle, I feel glad that they're actually doing something with it, because it is such a lovely building. We were actually invited over there when they first were going to take it over and it was just a shell basically. They hadn't done anything inside to it. I can remember what classrooms were what and where the assembly halls were and everything. It was really nice.

Jane Duffy

I'm not really sure yet about the new use of the school. I'm a bit anxious about the building at the back, all the residential stuff. I'm not too sure how that's going to work out with what's happening at the front. I want to see something happen there that's worthwhile. It will depend such a lot on whoever is in charge there, that person has got to be absolutely the right person. It could be a terrible flop and it could be a wonderful success. Some people wanted to see some form of museum or something like that there. It might be nice to have some archive stuff there. It's got to be manned, hasn't it? I was a little bit relieved when I actually realised that the residential bit was not going to be in the actual building, in the old part, because I couldn't see at first how that was going to work. But I can now see how it's intended to work, and I hope it does work.

If the youngsters can get the right support then it could be good. If they don't, it could become a den of iniquity; it could go all wrong. Voluntary work is fine and it's great that people go in and help out, but it's got to have a core of somebody who is actually responsible and carries the can at the end and who isn't just a volunteer being pushed beyond their limits. It wants somebody qualified and officially in charge and with a firm hand and then it will be fine.

I quite want to go in and have a look and see what they've done! I get a bit anxious about the old tunnel affair that goes under the front where the river runs under. If you go to Broad Street and you'll see the river disappears. It goes under the front there and it goes under what used to be the front playground and it comes out behind the Wool Pack. I sometimes get a bit worried about what's going to happen to all that if we get a lot of heavy traffic, because it must go under that junction somewhere there. I just hope they've done their homework.

Hazel Smith

It's being used for the wrong purpose. That would have made a nice cottage hospital. If you break your wrist or anything, we've either got to go to Bury or Cambridge. Where, if that was a cottage hospital, you could have it done here. Or a bit of it could be made into a maternity ward instead of ladies having to go to Cambridge to have their children. That would have been ideal. If you haven't got a car, the buses don't always run in times with the hospital, so sometimes you don't have visitors.

Percy Sizer

Whenever I've driven past, either just after it shut and it was all boarded up and now when they're redeveloping it, I always think "aah", I never go past thinking, "God, I hated that school" or think nothing at all. I always think something when I go past the Cangle.

You can still see it looks right from the front, but it's only that front block that's actually still there, isn't it? The dining area has all gone, the area where the pottery was and the kindergarten bit that was fronted on Wratting Road next to the dentist, that's all gone as well. If you look at the school from the front, it looks the same. When you go round the back, it's only basically that front block that's actually still there, the rest has gone. It's very sad.

Karen Clark

I think it's great to keep the building there. That really is important. It would have been a great shame to knock it down and do something else. If you think about that corner, it really dominates the corner. And so many people there have been through the Cangle School, so socially it's important. But also it really is quite an important site. I think they're doing a really good job with the appearance of it. And the use as well, there's definitely a need for single people housing in the town. So it's good on two grounds really.

Gerry Kiernan

I'd like to have a look round and have a nose inside. I'm intrigued to see what they've done. It looks fascinating. It looks absolutely brilliant from outside. I walk past it and just can't stop admiring it. People who are in the town recently, they just think it's a tremendous building. They've done a superb job. I love the carving they've done and tidied up all the stonework. I didn't know they were going to put the railings back. To see those going back, I was quite pleased.

Jane Farrow

I think it's great, because I think it's been ever so sad for the last few years when it's all been standing empty with all the windows broken and the boards up and I think it's really, really good that it's now going to be put to a good use and that people are going to have a chance to live here and have a new start, I think that's tremendous, a really good idea. When you come into Haverhill from Bury or Cambridge, it's really the first big building that you see and instead of it looking all tatty as it has done the last few years, it's going to look really lovely, so I think when people see that and all the good things that have gone inside, I think that's going to be good for Haverhill.

Geoffrey Ship

I think it's a good idea. It might save someone actually being homeless. It's a big job isn't it, leaving home?

Julie Smith

I think it's brilliant.

Peter Isaacs